Architecture-Based 5G Security Simulation

William S. Patel

Abstract

The fifth-generation technology standard for mobile networks (5G) introduced a massive increase in capability due to the increased use of Internet of Things devices. However, implementing additional untrusted technology, such as IoT devices, exposes the infrastructure to unsecure hardware and software. As a result, the attack surface of the 5G mobile network has increased after transitioning from LTE to the 5G standard. Three research questions and hypotheses were composed to evaluate the architectural design of the network for the healthcare use case. The Perimeter Security, Zero Trust

Microsegmentation, and Non-Standalone Models were designed in the Cyber Virtual Assured Network simulator so that the researcher can identify the ideal architectural solution. The researcher composed three research questions that are concerned with the effectiveness of the 5G topology design, the security resilience of a simulated cyber architecture, and architecture model comparison in network latency performance. For the hypotheses, the author conducted research to substantiate that the User Equipment-New Radio is the most effective topology in completing the scope of work, CyberVAN can enhance the security resilience of the 5G network, and the Perimeter Security Model performs best in network latency. After comparing the models, the researcher concluded the Zero Trust

Microsegmentation Model is the most cyber-resilient architecture for the healthcare use case that performed well in network latency performance. Lastly, the author recommends future work for other researchers who show interest in this research

Table of Contents

Chapter 1—Introduction

1.1 Background

The fifth-generation technology standard for mobile networks (5G) was deployed by Industry about five years ago but needs to be properly secured. Kight (2023) states,

"5G mobile connectivity is expected to add nearly $1 trillion to the global economy by 2030, with almost half of this coming from new enterprise services and apps, across sectors including finance, healthcare, and education." The larger amount of user devices connected to the 5G mobile network contributes to the costly connectivity expansion around the globe. In addition, the virtualization of the mobile network's infrastructure applies to some applications of 5G communications, which also contributes to the expensive deployment of 5G networks. Cybersecurity challenges are greater for 5G due to the expanded attack surface, which sophisticates the security control implementation and risk management responsibilities.

The researcher acknowledges that sustaining and protecting 5G is an essential mission since it is a part of the nation's critical infrastructure. In turn, federal agencies such as the Cybersecurity and Infrastructure Security Agency (CISA), Department of Homeland Security (DHS), National Institute of Standards and Technology (NIST),

National Security Agency (NSA), and National Telecommunications and Information Administration (NTIA) communicate the need to better protect our mobile network infrastructure now than ever before due to 5G's enhanced capabilities. Improved performance and device expansion are the most significant benefits of transitioning to 5G communications, but the negative implication of these enhancements is a larger attack surface. Federal publications such as the 2023 National Cybersecurity Strategy, CISA 5G Strategy, National Strategy to Secure 5G, 5G Impacts on Cybersecurity, and 5G Cybersecurity: Preparing a Secure Evolution to 5G elaborates on the vulnerabilities of the 5G infrastructure, and what initiatives are currently in place to protect the network. Furthermore, the cyber resilience of 5G technology will be discussed in this Praxis and are sourced by some of the corporate leaders in the cybersecurity industry.

1.2 Research Motivation

The motivation behind this research is the importance of maintaining a cyberresilient critical infrastructure in the United States. DHS (2023) in the "Secure Cyberspace and Critical Infrastructure" states, "the critical infrastructure provides services that are the backbone of the American people's economic security, health, and well-being." The source further explains that the cybersecurity threats to critical infrastructure are risks to the United States that threaten the nation's security, safety, etc. The Department of State (2019) in "5G Security" adds to the conversation and says that 5G will enhance public services for nations around the world, and nations must prioritize the cyber protection of 5G networks because threat actors are discovering tactics, techniques, and procedures (TTPs) in exploiting 5G communications.

The concerns from the federal authorizers of 5G regarding its overall security posture also motivated the researcher to choose this topic. DHS

(2023) in “Secure Cyberspace and Critical Infrastructure” mentions that cyber attackers’ Tactics, Techniques, and Procedures (TTPs) could cause major disruptions to 5G services now that threat actors have more tools, entry points, and vulnerabilities to leverage. Moreover, NIS Corporation Group (2019) states the following about cyber risks associated with the 5G mobile network: “Their number and significance is likely to increase with 5G, due to the increased level of complexity of the technology and of the future greater reliance of economies and societies on this infrastructure.”

Lastly, the researcher was motivated to conduct this research topic after learning about the Department of Defense’s vision in implementing the Zero Trust (ZT) strategy throughout its enterprises. This strategy is one that is encouraged by Industry and federal authorities such as the Department of Defense (DoD). Because 5G is an essential part of the critical infrastructure, a strategy such as Zero Trust that enforces security within perimeter borders is necessary. Pimplaskar (2022) states that Zero Trust Architectures (ZTAs) will be important in securing the new frontier of 5G critical infrastructure. These architectures will help organizations meet the latest security requirements and keep pace with challenges associated with the expanded attack surface.

1.3 Problem Statement

The implementation of additional untrusted technology into the 5G network exposes the infrastructure to unsecure and malicious hardware and software, such as an Internet of Things (IoT) cyberattack, which causes an average of $250K in corporate losses for each incident (Passett, 2023).

This research will address the implementation of additional untrusted technology into the 5G network that exposes the infrastructure to unsecure and malicious hardware and software (CISA, 2023). Simpson and Wheeler (2019) states, "The after-the-fact cost of missing a proactive 5G cybersecurity opportunity will be much greater than the cost of cyber diligence upfront." The nation must create conditions by which 5G subscribers can make intelligent cybersecurity decisions upfront. The attack surface of the 5G network has increased after transitioning from the Long-Term Evolution (LTE) infrastructure due to enhanced capabilities. High adoption of IoT devices by users presents new vulnerabilities despite the network slicing ability of 5G and exposes the infrastructure to many distinct attack vectors.

Keyfactor, a cybersecurity company specializing in digital asset protection through encryption and authentication, alongside Vanson Bourne released new statistics after examining the state of IoT security of end users and manufacturers (Passett, 2023). The study surveyed 1200 IoT experts and professionals across the globe from many different countries in the Western and Eastern hemispheres. The significant findings recorded in the survey are that 97% of organizations struggle to protect IoT devices, and 89% of surveyors' organizations actively using IoT products were attacked by threat actors at an average cost of $250K for each incident. Proper education and security guidance are necessary for industries to understand that security must be "baked" into
IoT design.

1.4 book Statement

A simulation-based security architecture will assist in mitigation recommendations for IoT devices connected to the 5G network.

Upon completion, this research will yield a security architecture design that effectively balances the security and performance of the 5G network through a business use case. This is a significant achievement, as it ensures that performance is not compromised. The deliverable format, snapshots of the testbed, is designed for easy access through a web portal. In addition, the actual testbed hosted on CyberVAN is also available upon request. The expected usage of the deliverable is that Industry implements architectural practices of this Praxis so that continuing research enhances the network's cyber resilience in the 5G Standalone (SA) topology and prepares for 6G deployment. The principal research methodology is Modeling & Simulation (M&S) and Data Analytics. The architecture input will be a selected packet capture dataset, and the outputs are security controls and security policy recommendations. The proposed security architecture will resolve the issue of untrusted technology currently implemented in the 5G network design. The deliverable is an architectural model for an emerging marketspace without a current standard to protect it.

1.5 Research Objectives

There are several research objectives that the author plans to satisfy after completing this Praxis. The ultimate objective is to develop and simulate a 5G cyber architecture through M&S means. However, the other architectural objectives of this Praxis are as follows:

- Evaluate the security profile of different 5G architecture models in the Cyber

  Virtual Assured Network (CyberVAN) simulator
- Assess the network latency results of each 5G architecture designed in CyberVAN and leverage statistical analysis to magnify the differences in the outcomes
- Encourage Industry to conduct extensive architectural research to enhance the mobile network's cyber resilience in preparation of 6G deployment

1.6 Research Questions and Hypotheses

To successfully conduct this research, the author must establish specific research questions and hypotheses before executing the methodology. The specific research questions and hypotheses that will clarify the purpose of this research are as follows:

RQ1: Which network topology (User Equipment-Radio Network Access, User

Equipment-New Radio) in CyberVAN is most effective in completing the scope of work?

RQ2: Can CyberVAN enhance the security resilience of the 5G architecture?

RQ3: Does the Perimeter Security, Zero Trust Microsegmentation, or Non-

Standalone Model perform better in network latency?

H1: The 5G User Equipment-New Radio topology in CyberVAN is most effective in completing the scope of work.

H2: CyberVAN will enhance the security resilience of the 5G architecture.

H3: The Perimeter Security Model performs better in network latency.

1.7 Scope of Research

The researcher will develop and simulate a 5G architecture through Modeling & Simulation (M&S) and data analytics to assess the network latency implications of unique cybersecurity architectures of differing security control implementation methodologies.

1.8 Research Limitations

A plethora of network simulators were available in the market; however, most simulation tools did not apply to the author's research topic for several reasons. The researcher assessed the network simulators in terms of network type consideration, scalability, and license cost, and the high cost was the primary consideration that prohibited the author from utilizing many simulation tool options. Availability was another factor that the author needed to consider during the simulator selection process. For example, OPNET was the researcher's first network simulation option, but later discovered that it was acquired by Riverbed, who did not release the software to the author. A point of contact from the Sales Department explained to the researcher that the Riverbed Modeler was a relatively new network simulator, which complicates the software release process of this novel product. Additionally, the Cisco Packet Tracer was highly coveted but was too elementary in its capabilities to accomplish the objectives of this research topic. As a result, Cyber Virtual Assured Network (CyberVAN) was selected as the simulator of choice, but it had some cyber resilience testing limitations that the researcher discovered during the research work, which will be explained in Chapter 4.

Another significant limitation is that the Praxis is only specific to the healthcare use case. Providing context to an architectural issue in cybersecurity is essential because it is impossible to generate a universal architectural solution for at least several industries. Unlike other industries, the healthcare sector consists of various types of sensitive data that will be discussed in further detail later in this Praxis. There may be similarities between healthcare and other use cases that consist of different sensitive data types; however, the ultimate architectural solution may be more stringent due to the Community Profile of healthcare. Lastly, the author is only concerned with the data throughput of the 5G New Radio (NR) User and Control Planes in conjunction with the Evolved Packet Core (EPC). The author will determine the ideal architecture solution for the healthcare industry by comparing the efficiency of two distinct simulation models.

1.9 Organization of Praxis

Chapter 1 of the Praxis is the Introduction that includes the following sections:

Research Background, Research Motivation, Problem Statement, book Statement,

Research Objectives, Research Questions and Hypotheses, Scope of Research, Research Limitations, and Organization of Praxis. Chapter 2 is the

Literature Review, where the author will summarize the main points of each source, analyze and interpret the source findings' significance of the source findings, and evaluate each source's strengths and weaknesses. Chapter 3 is the Methodology section that elaborates on why the researcher selected the chosen procedures and techniques in conducting the architectural research. Chapter 4 is the Results section, where the applied research outcomes are demonstrated, and the findings of the study that test the author's research hypotheses are reported. Chapter 5 is the Conclusion and will provide details on why the public should find the author's research significant. The conclusion will also include the researcher's suggested architecture solution for the business use case and future work recommendations.

Chapter 2—Literature Review

2.1 Introduction

The discussion about protecting the critical infrastructure of the United States has been a hot topic for several years. On February 12, 2014, President Obama introduced the Cybersecurity Framework, which according to the White House (2014), "Results from a year-long private-sector-led effort to develop a voluntary how-to guide for organizations in the critical infrastructure community to enhance their cybersecurity." The Cybersecurity Framework is the product of the Executive Order titled "Improving Critical Infrastructure Cybersecurity" (The White House, 2014). The White House (2013) states, "The critical infrastructure consists of systems and assets, whether physical or virtual, and are so vital to the United States that the incapacity or destruction of such systems and assets would have a debilitating impact on security, national economic security, national public health, and safety."

Vargas and Tien (2023) affirm that the 5G mobile network will change the way information is transmitted throughout the critical infrastructure. Additionally, 5G will enable other technologies to perform continuous system monitoring, such as artificial intelligence, to accomplish high efficiency (Vargas & Tien, 2023, para. 1). Federal Government and Industry publications confirm how essential 5G is to enable the growth of critical infrastructure. However, the primary challenge is to secure the mobile network as its capabilities and influence to enhance other technologies expand.

This chapter will elaborate on the 5G mobile network security challenges cited from various publications such as articles, journals, and federal documents. The Literature Review is divided into nine elements: Introduction, Title Searches, Articles, Federal Publications, Journals, 5G Overview, Zero Trust Strategy, Network Simulation, and the Conclusion.

2.2 Sources

The researcher read through 143 peer-reviewed informational news, journal articles, and federal publications for this research. The selection process involved the author researching website content and many article sources that are pertinent to the Praxis topic. In addition, the researcher selected several official federal publications released by organizations such as the Cybersecurity and Infrastructure Security Agency (CISA), Department of Commerce (DoC), Department of Energy (DoE), Department of Homeland Security (DHS), Department of Defense (DoD), National Institute of Standards and Technology (NIST), National Telecommunications and Information Administration (NTIA), etc. Some of these federal publications include DoD Directives (DoDD), Department of Defense Instructions (DoDI), and documents that explain specific DoD processes and procedures. Several non-DoD publications governing the cyber resilience of federal systems and critical infrastructure were also reviewed and referenced in this Praxis.

2.3 5G Overview

The 5G wireless standard offers higher upload and download speeds and transforms how society utilizes the Internet to access applications, social networks, and corporate data. However, there are many attack vectors that cyber attackers could exploit. To better protect our critical infrastructure and the devices on them, we need to identify as many vulnerabilities as we can so they can be addressed. Christopher Krebs, former CISA Director, stated the following statement according to the "CISA 5G Strategy:
Ensuring the Security and Resilience of 5G Infrastructure In Our Nation": "5G is the single biggest critical infrastructure build that the globe has seen in the last 25 years and, coupled with the growth of cloud computing, automation, and future of artificial intelligence, demands focused attention today to secure tomorrow." The stakes for protecting the nation's critical data networks are at an all-time high since a greater number of user devices will connect to the Internet, which exposes the critical infrastructure to cyber espionage attacks (CISA, 2020, p. 1).

One of the federal publications under review is the "CISA 5G Strategy: Ensuring the Security and Resilience of 5G Infrastructure in Our Nation". CISA is under DHS, and its purpose is to enhance the security of the nation's physical infrastructure. The strategy is closely tied with the "National Strategy to Secure 5G", which was composed by the White House and outlines the four Lines of Effort (LOEs) designated in the "CISA 5G Strategy: Ensuring the Security and Resilience of 5G Infrastructure in Our Nation".

These four LOEs establish the five strategic initiatives to secure the 5G network.

According to the National Strategy to Secure 5G, the four LOEs are as follows:

- "Facilitate Domestic 5G Rollout" (The White House, 2020, p. 2)
- "Assess Risks and Identify Core Security Principles of 5G Infrastructure" (The White House, 2020, p. 3)
- "Address Risks to United States Economic and National Security During Development and Deployment of 5G Infrastructure Worldwide" (The White House, 2020, p. 4-5)
- "Promote Responsible Global Development and Deployment of 5G" (The White House, 2020, pp. 6-7)

CISA (2020), in the "CISA 5G Strategy: Ensuring the Security and Resilience of 5G Infrastructure In Our Nation," states, "Each of the strategic initiatives address critical risks to secure 5G deployment, such as physical security concerns, attempts by threat actors to influence the design and architecture of the network, vulnerabilities within the 5G supply chain, and an increased attack surface for malicious actors to exploit weaknesses (p. 6)". The five strategic initiatives (SIs) are shown below:

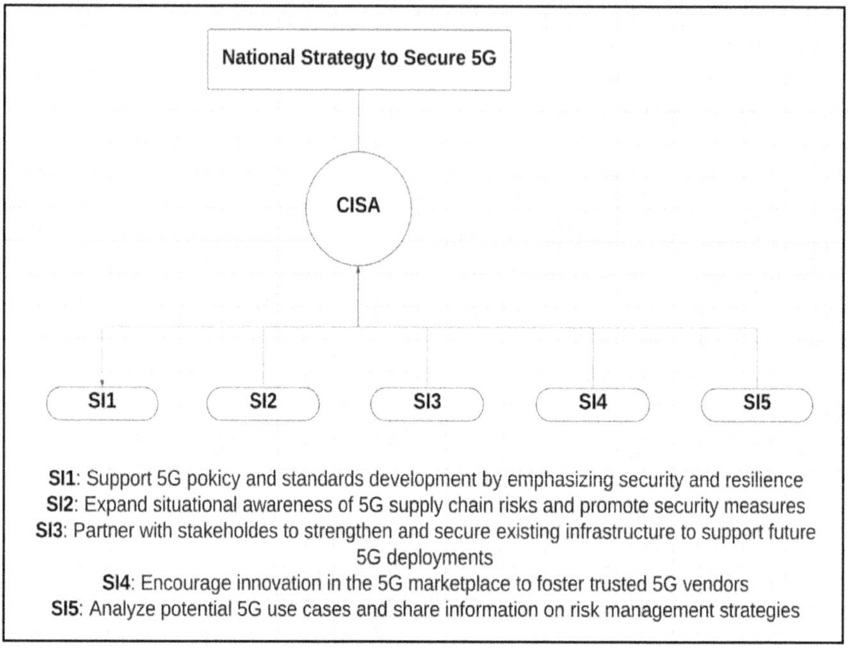

Figure 1. CISA's Five Strategic Initiatives and their Descriptions (adapted from

CISA, 2020, p. 6).

"The National Strategy to Secure 5G" was developed by the White House in March 2020, and its accompanying Implementation Plan composed by NTIA was released in January

2021.

One of the topologies is the 5G NSA deployment. NIST (2020), in "5G Cybersecurity - Preparing a Secure Evolution to 5G," defines this configuration as utilizing the 5G NR with the EPC without launching a new virtualized core network (p.

6). The NSA topology is illustrated below:

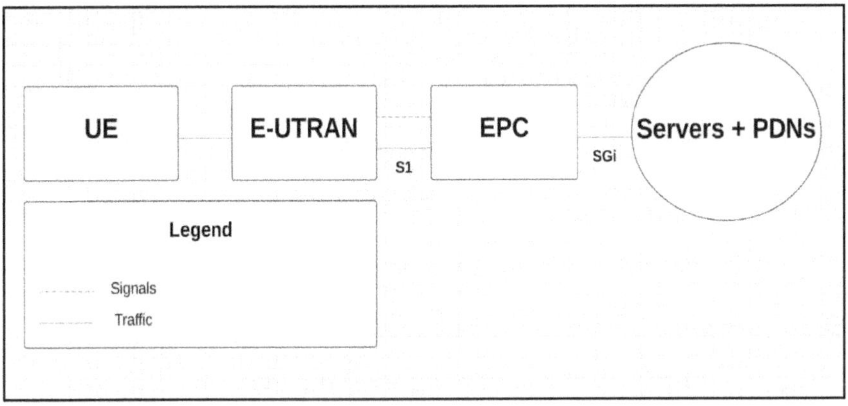

Figure 2. 5G System with Non-Standalone Core Network (adapted from Tutorialspoint, n.d.).

The Evolved Universal Terrestrial Radio Access Network (E-UTRAN) is another name designation for the Radio Access Network (RAN) that is described throughout this Praxis. "S1" is the interface between the RAN and the EPC to enable communication between the UE network segment and the Internet. "SGi" is the interface between the PC and the Internet. The architecture models showcased in Chapter 4 consist of the SGW, PGW, and MME network functions that assemble the EPC. The PGW exchanges data with the Internet through the SGi interface, and the SGW routes data packets from the RAN to the PGW through the S1 interface (Tutorialspoint, n.d., paras. 12-13). The MME manages the mobility of user devices within the network by tracking their location and state. It also handles signaling between the UE and the network and the Evolved Node B (eNB) and CN (Tutorialspoint, n.d., para. 14).

Bartock et al. (2020) state that the 5G NSA topology incorporates the benefits of utilizing the 5G NR without launching a new virtualized core network, whereas the SA system implements core network virtualization (pp. 5-6). The objective of 5G NSA topology is to design the EPC's cybersecurity features that demonstrate a strong security posture in the 5G NSA topology (Bartock et al., 2020, p. 7). Awati (n.d.) elaborates on the network elements of the EPC. The components that construct the EPC are the Mobile Management Entity (MME), Serving Gateway (SGW), Packet Data Network Gateway (PGW), and Policy and Charging Rules Function (PCRF). The MME performs session management responsibilities, controls user network access with the Home Subscriber Server (HSS), and monitors user state and location (Awati, n.d., para. 9). The SGW connects the 5G Radio Access Network (RAN) to the EPC and serves as a router in forwarding packets through the RAN to the EPC (Awati, n.d., para. 10). Awati (n.d.) states that the PGW is the interface for the 5GS to connect to the Internet by routing packets between the internal and external networks and performing packet inspection and user IP address allocation duties (para. 11). Lastly, the PCRF performs policy enforcement and billing record generation called flow-based charging, enforced for paid services in a client-user relationship (Awati, n.d., para. 12).

The other 5G topology is the SA deployment. CISA (2020) in the "CISA 5G Strategy: Ensuring the Security and Resilience of 5G Infrastructure in Our Nation" states that the 5G SA network will take years to implement and deploy. The source continues, "However, transitioning to a SA network will allow end-users to realize the full potential of 5G, enabling applications that require connectivity for tens of billions of devices over large areas, ultra-low latency for critical near-real-time communications, and faster, more reliable connections in crowded areas." The 5G SA CN, also known as the Service-Based Architecture (SBA), is entirely software-based, allowing for greater flexibility on cloud infrastructures (Ericsson, n.d., para. 3). Dryjanski illustrates the 5G System (5GS) below:

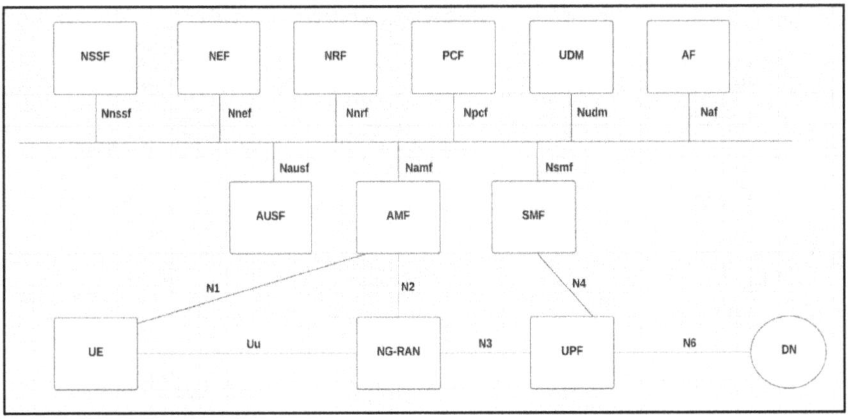

Figure 3. 5G System with the Standalone Core Network (adapted from Dryjanski,

2018).

The 5G Standalone core network is illustrated in Figure 3 and utilizes more network elements that encompass functions of the Evolved Packet Core in a service-based architecture (SBA).

The SBA evolved from the EPC by changing the Control and User Plane Separation (CUPS) functions into cloud-based services, which are provided via a communication protocol over a network. They are web-based Application Programming Interfaces (APIs) that implement an agile deployment of the core services. This design enhances the modularity of the network elements, and the service-oriented architecture is now not confined to specific vendors, products, and technologies (Lekshmi, 2024).

None of the above 5GC functions exist in CyberVAN, but the 4G LTE elements are available for implementation in CyberVAN. Therefore, the researcher decided to construct the 5G cyber architecture using the LTE CN elements, i.e., 5G NSA, due to CyberVAN's limited capabilities. Despite this limitation, Section 2.6 supported the claim that CyberVAN was the best network simulation tool option for the scope of work (SoW), which is detailed in Chapter 1 after weighing network type consideration, scalability, and license cost. However, it is important to note that this problem would have existed if the researcher had selected a different network simulation tool because the industry has not caught up with today's plan for deploying the 5G SA core architecture.

This topology incorporates the NR base stations like NSA; however, the core network is re-designed as a software-driven, cloud-native, and service-based architecture. This new 5G Core (5GC) is also known as the Service-Based Architecture (SBA) and consists of many network functions that are interconnected via a service bus to expose the network capabilities inside and outside of the 5GC. Pathak (2020) describes the network functions (NFs) of the 5GS as follows:

- Access and Mobility Management Function (AMF): It is similar to the MME and is the only point of entry for the user equipment–delegates to the Session

Management Function (SMF) to control the context of user sessions (Pathak, 2020, para. 12)

- Application Function (AF): Expose services to end users, retrieve resources, and communicate with the PCF for policy control, among other things (Pathak, 2020, para. 20)
- Authentication Server Function (AUSF): This network element is similar to the Home Subscriber Server (HSS) and delegates to the AMF to authenticate UE traffic (Pathak, 2020, para. 13).
- Network Exposure Function (NEF): Utilizes Application Programming Interfaces (APIs) both inside and outside the 5G Core (5GC) to provide resources and services (Pathak, 2020, para. 16).
- NF Repository Function (NRF): Tracks available NF instances and their corresponding profiles. It also registers and delivers services so that distinct NFs can find one another using Application Programming Interfaces (APIs) (Pathak, 2020, para. 17).
- Network Slice Selection Function (NSSF): Tracks instances of network slices that an operator specifies and routes traffic to the appropriate network slice (Pathak, 2020, para. 15).
- Policy Control Function (PCF): Utilizes subscription data and policy decisions to control network activity (Pathak, 2020, para. 18).
- Session Management Function (SMF): This element's function is similar to the activities of SGW, PGW, and MME. Performs UE IP

allocation and controls the context of user sessions (Pathak, 2020, para. 14).

- Unified Data Management (UDM): Its features are similar to those of the HSS. Handles user identification, manages subscriptions, authenticates users, and grants access (Pathak, 2020, para. 19).
- User Plane Function (UPF): Its features compare to the SGW and PGW, and is in charge of policy enforcement, packet inspection, among other things (Pathak, 2020, para. 11).

Pathak (2020) continues that the SBA provides the necessary flexibility, agility, and scalability to expose 5G services by constructing a cloud-native architecture (para. 21).

This is the first iteration of the mobile network standard, where virtualized network functions, network softwarization, cloud-native applications, and network capability exposure over service bus and application programming interfaces (APIs) exist.

The benefits of 5G NSA regarding efficiency are reduced costs, easy deployment, and fast rollout. With 5G NSA, network operators can construct the 5G network on top of the existing 4G LTE by leveraging the EPC. This reduces both cost and time by utilizing the EPC and avoiding extensive work in implementing a new 5G core network. Easy deployment is another benefit of using the 5G NSA topology since the network operators are already familiar with the EPC infrastructure, which eases the 5G New Radio (NR) configuration process. In turn, a fast rollout of the 5G network is imminent because the network operators will use the EPC for internal and external network routing responsibilities. However, the 5G SA network includes the 5G Radio Access Network (RAN) and a new cloud-native core network. Network operators must configure the new core architecture while learning to manage it over time. Carriers and network operators elected to launch 5G NSA systems as the SA core, also known as the Service-Based Architecture (SBA), matures in technological readiness. SA has several benefits that justify its deployment worthiness, including reduced power consumption. Less power will be consumed since there is only one network connectivity method after EPC removal (Tech Target, 2024). However, the main disadvantage of 5G SA is the costly job of implementing the comprehensive SBA network functions that were described earlier in this section. Additionally, the SA is more time-consuming than the NSA network since training is required for operators to learn the new SA core. Both topologies will be discussed further in Chapters 3 and 4.

2.4 Perimeter Security Strategy

Perimeter security is a traditional concept that has existed since the notion of protecting network resources was first introduced. It acts as the first and only line of defense if there does not exist a Defense-in-Depth (DiD) approach. US Signal (2021) states, "The main idea behind DiD is that if any security control protecting critical systems or information is compromised, another control is in place to stop or limit the impact of the attack" (para. 3). DiD, also known as "layered security," integrates various security controls that can be applied in addition to the perimeter firewall to protect network resources from threat actors on external networks.

In the traditional perimeter firewall model, trust exists inside the network boundary but is non-existent outside of it. TUCU (2021) states, "Perimeter security is a philosophy that involves setting up functional devices, tools, and techniques around the boundary of a network to secure its data and resources. It is one facet of the greater security field and is vital in active system protection." (para. 28). The Perimeter Security (PS) Model demonstrates an internal network protected along its border by a firewall that can be considered either the perimeter firewall, external firewall, or edge firewall. Additionally, it demonstrates a single point of failure, which is not what the researcher suggests for the healthcare use case, especially considering that many corporations in the industry have already been breached due to the lack of high prioritization for the cybersecurity mission. For example, the Elitecare Emergency Hospital in League City, Texas, recently experienced a network server data breach, and the breach report filing date is September 18, 2024 (Console, 2024, para. 1). The report was submitted to the Secretary of the Department of Health and Human Services (HHS) for admitting to unsecured Protected Health Information (PHI), which is a direct violation of the Health Insurance Portability and Accountability Act (HIPAA). The number of individuals affected by this breach is currently 24,754 (Alder, 2024, para. 1). Many of the healthcare sector's Information Technology (IT) systems do not implement diversity, which is a practice that prevents the risk of single point of failure exploitation by enforcing the same security control more than once in a cybersecurity architecture.

In terms of cost and complexity, the PS Model is less expensive in upfront costs since it requires fewer changes to network architecture. PS cost considerations include hardware or software costs of physical security devices such as firewalls, ongoing licensing costs of security solutions, maintenance support such as hardware or software replacements, and scalability requirements to increase PS devices as the network grows. According to Fortinet (2024) in "Network Firewall Price: Comparing Security Costs", hardware firewalls for small firms can cost between $700 and $1000, while larger organizations up to 100 users should anticipate paying between $1500 and $4000 (para. 5). An additional factor that can drive up the cost of hardware firewalls, according to Fortinet (2024), is the make, model, and characteristics of the firewalls (para. 5). Nonetheless, the PS Model utilizes only one firewall to defend the network boundary, so the upfront cost is fairly inexpensive compared to other security architecture models.

In terms of security, the PS model is less secure since there is only one defense mechanism protecting the internal network. In other words, the PS model does not practice diversity and redundancy. Diversity is where several distinct security controls are implemented in an architecture to enhance security resilience, but redundancy protects the network by eliminating a single point of failure. If a cybercriminal manages to get past this one barrier, the perimeter firewall is the only point of failure. This is where the ZT comes into play. Diversity and redundancy exist in ZT since multiple security controls are implemented in case one fails to defend critical assets against the attacker. Marks (2021), in "Cyberresilience in an Evolving Threat Landscape, " defines diversity as "the use of heterogeneity to minimize common mode failures, particularly threat events exploiting common vulnerabilities." The source continues by stating the following about redundancy: "Provides multiple protected instances of critical resources."

A perimeter network that protects an internal network from unauthorized traffic is called a demilitarized zone, or DMZ (Zenarmor, n.d., para. 11). The DMZ concept is another tactic in designing perimeter security, and the end goal of this network is to access external networks while keeping the internal network secure. The DMZ houses servers that offer the following services: Domain Name System (DNS), File Transfer Protocol (FTP), web, mail, proxy, Voice over Internet (VoIP), etc. Fortinet (n.d.) in "DMZ Networks" states, "A DMZ network provides a buffer between the Internet and an organization's private network. The DMZ is isolated by a security gateway, such as a firewall, that filters traffic between the DMZ and a LAN. Another security gateway that filters traffic from external networks protects the default DMZ server. It is located between two firewalls, and the DMZ firewall setup ensures incoming network packets are observed by a firewall—or other security tools—before they make it through to the servers hosted in the DMZ" (para. 5-6). If a threat actor can compromise a DMZ system after penetrating the external firewall, the attacker still needs to penetrate the internal firewall to access sensitive data.

2.5 Zero Trust Strategy

Before "Zero Trust" was officially dubbed as the term for the concept by cybersecurity experts, the Defense Information Systems Agency (DISA) and DoD established "black core" as the de-perimeterization of cyber defense. "Black core" was about instilling security for individual nodes and transactions, which is today's "Zero Trust" ultimate objective. Rose et al. (2020) in "Zero Trust Architecture" states, "the Jericho Forum in 2004 publicized the concept of de-perimeterization—limiting implicit trust based on network location and the limitations of relying on single, static defenses over a large network segment. De-perimeterization evolved into the notion of ZT, which was coined by John Kindervag while at Forrester. Zero Trust then became the term used to describe solutions that moved security away from implied trust based on network location and instead focused on evaluating trust on a per-transaction basis" (p. 2). The ZT approach focuses on safeguarding resources such as assets, services, workflows, and network accounts and does not prioritize network location as the top component of a system's security posture.

Additionally, ZT allows for the protection of all assets, including devices, applications, etc. Rose et al. (2020) states, "ZT is not a single architecture but a set of guiding principles for workflow, system design, and operations that can be used to improve the security posture of any classification or sensitivity level" (p. 1). The ZT principles create an overarching framework, but the complete removal of implicit trust is a new mindset to establish. The seven tenets of ZT are shown below:

NIST's Seven Tenets of Zero Trust
T1. All data sources and computing resources are considered resources.
T2. All communication is secured regardless of network location.
T3. Access to individual resources is granted on a per-session basis.
T4. Access to resources is determined by dynamic policy - including the observable state of client identity, application/service, and the requesting asset - and may include other behavioral and environmental attributes.
T5. The operator monitors and measures the integrity and security posture of all owned and associated assets.
T6. All resource authentication and authorization are dynamic and strictly enforced before access is allowed.
T7. The operator collects as much information as possible about the current state of assets, network infrastructure, and communications and uses it to improve its security posture.

Table 1. Seven Tenets of Zero Trust (adapted from NIST, 2020, pp. 6-7).

According to NIST Special Publication 800-207, the ZT tenets remove the concept of network perimeter defense, also known as the Perimeter Security Model.

The ZT Microsegmentation Model demands more upfront investment due to additional architectural changes and expertise. Furthermore, ZT is fairly new as a cybersecurity strategy, so every healthcare worker, including management, must be trained in ensuring compliance with ZT principles and practices. Initial implementation will require expert consulting to assess the architecture and its policies. Training is a security control that will drive up costs significantly for this model since continuous monitoring of Information

Assurance (IA) is essential to ensure compliance with ZT policy. This is known as management complexity. Other considerations of the ZT Microsegmentation Model that drive up ongoing costs include hardware or software licensing, policy enforcement management, and software microsegmentation tools, if applicable, such as Cisco Secure Workload, Illumio, and VMware NSX. There is a proportional relationship between the upfront cost and the complexity of an architecture.

Again, architecture consists of the three elements: people, process, and technology. Several factors, such as organization size and infrastructure complexity, significantly increase upfront costs, which suggests that a larger healthcare corporation such as the Johns Hopkins Health System (JHHS) would spend more money to implement the PS or ZT Microsegmentation Models in comparison to a smaller corporation.

Microsegmentation is a key security technique in the ZTA. It is a method that divides a larger network into segments while applying security controls to each segment. In other words, this ZT component isolates workloads from one another, which creates secure zones within an architecture design. By creating secure zones, the organization is able to reduce the attack surface and improve breach containment. Adversarial lateral movement is prevented after an organization secures each zone, which will contain the cyber attacker only in the breached zone. Another advantage of this technique is the traffic limitation benefit. Firewall policies will limit east-west network traffic between network segments. The ZT Microsegmentation Model costs more upfront; however, there are reports from Chief Information Security Officers

(CISOs) that suggest significant cost savings over time. Below is the projected cost savings that AirGap in 2024 reported from CISOs:

Microsegmentation Benefit	Savings Per Year
No more endpoint software agent requirements reducing IT Help Desk time and costs	$187000
Improving network visibility, control, and asset access using Multi-Factor Authentication (MFA) and Single Sign-On	$360000
No more trial-and-error defense techniques against intrusion attempts that incurred overtime rates for IT and cybersecurity teams	$106250
Eliminating network zones and reducing hardware, software, servicing licensing, and maintenance costs	$54000
Reducing risk of fines and regulatory action by consistently enforcing security controls (including legal fees to contest HIPAA violations)	$25000
Value of Microsegmentation Benefits Based on CISO's Cost Estimates	$732250

Table 2. Cost Savings of Microsegmentation Benefits (adapted from Agrawal,n.d.). Table 2 highlights the benefits of the ZT Microsegmentation Model with the projected cost savings per year using an AirGap ZT Everywhere solution.

The assumption here is that the solution would cost $150,000 a year, but the total Return on Investment (ROI) based on the figures above would yield a return of $4.88 for every dollar invested. The ROI was calculated by dividing the total cost estimates, which is $732,250, by the estimated cost of microsegmentation per year, or $150,000. The quotient is $4.88 as the return on every dollar invested, which substantiates the benefit of implementing the ZT Microsegmentation Model, according to the AirGap report. The above figures are from CISOs of mid-size and large-scale enterprises who requested anonymity due to the data's confidential nature. The bottom line, according to the anonymous CISOs in the report, is that the ZT Microsegmentation Model will pay for itself within months of preventing security breaches at a rate of $4.88 in value for every dollar spent. AirGap (2024) states these additional factors in implementing the ZT Microsegmentation Model:

- Microsegmentation ROI estimates can fluctuate, and it is best to get started with a microsegmentation pilot to capture live data with budgets available at the end of the quarter since organizations usually allocate the remaining cybersecurity budgets at the end of a quarter
- Define and measure microsegmentation initiatives' progress in accomplishing the organization's goals and objectives using a cyber dashboard that is accessible at anytime

Cost and complexity are closely tied together since they have a proportional relationship, but from a complexity standpoint, the ZT Microsegmentation Model was found to be more complex in its architecture design than the Perimeter Security Model by the researcher. This is because network segmentation is further implemented since the perimeter of individual network elements is protected, unlike the UE network segment in the PS Model. The ZT Microsegmentation Model utilizes the same perimeter firewall to defend external network traffic but implements enhanced security by configuring additional security mechanisms to microsegment the UE network. The configured firewalls at neighboring nodes can facilitate the containment of the attacker and execute the pre-established Incident Response (IR) playbook. This approach is also known as diversity, which yields a more granular architecture for enhanced security. In Chapters 35, this ZT technique will be compared to the PS strategy to assess system implications of each architecture. There are other ZT approaches designated by NIST SP 800-207, such as enhanced identity governance and software-defined infrastructure applications. Resource access rules for the enhanced identity governance technique are determined by user and identity characteristics. Other confidence level factors that influence resource access decisions are devices used and asset classification. This strategy is employed using an enterprise network with visitor access. Initially, access is granted to all users until one requests access to a resource and is restricted to an identity with the appropriate access privileges. Enhanced identity governance is applicable when identity access management (IAM) technologies and techniques are used. For the purpose of this Praxis, this model would not serve as the best option since none of the network simulation tool options contained an IAM system as a network element. According to "Zero Trust

Architecture", ZTA implementation is achieved using an overlay network for the software-defined infrastructure approach (pp. 12-13). Software Defined Networks (SDNs) are frequently used in this model and facilitate the establishment of a secure communication channel between the client and resource (p. 13). This approach would be ideal for the 5G SA topology since the CN is a service-based architecture (SBA) but would not be applicable in a 5G NSA simulation environment.

2.6 Network Simulation

Several network simulation tools were considered for use in this research topic. While researching the available network simulation software currently on the market, certain factors were determined based on the desired results of the Praxis. These factors include network type consideration, learning curve, scalability, and license cost. Some tools are better suited for network applications such as enterprise, mobile networks, cloud-based systems, etc. The learning curve for each tool will differ due to the software's ease of use and complexity. Network size capability and overall tool complexity equals scalability, which is considered to ensure that the software can meet the 5G mobile network requirements. Lastly, licensing cost is essential because the researcher must establish the cost threshold for purchasing the tool. In this case, the researcher sought out free and open-source or inexpensive software with adequate capabilities and functionality to conduct the Praxis research. The researcher considered the following tools: Cisco Packet Tracer, CyberVAN, NetSim, OPNET, and Riverbed Modeler.

Cisco Packet Tracer is a network simulator, but a learning program created by

Cisco for beginners interested in earning cyber certifications. This tool is used in Cisco's Networking Academy and offers realistic elements of an actual network. The benefit of the Cisco Packet Tracer is that it offers a simulation environment that hosts virtual equipment and possesses the ability to view internal processes and network traffic in real time. Several Internet sources mentioned this Cisco tool as one of the best on the market; however, Packet Tracer is best used for educational purposes. This tool's network type consideration and application differs from what the researcher needs in the simulation software. Furthermore, the Cisco Packet Tracer is a network simulator used by students and professionals interested in earning the Cisco Certified Network Associate (CCNA) certification, which is considered an entry-level achievement. However, researchers utilized Packet Tracer to conduct 5G and IoT research analysis and implementation, such as Gurjar and Dangra (2022). Their research concentrated on analyzing and implementing smart residential buildings using the network simulator in 2022. Packet Tracer is a free simulation and open-source tool, but only for CCNA certification exam preparation purposes. Additionally, one must enroll in the Introduction to Cisco Packet Tracer and CCNA courses to gain access to the software. Despite this software's many benefits, the researcher determined that it is not an ideal tool of choice for this research.

Peraton Labs (n.d.) in "CyberVAN: Cyber Virtual Assured Network" states, "Cyber Virtual Assured Network (CyberVAN) provides the highest possible fidelity representation of a network by representing the network in a discrete event network simulator and enabling hosts, represented by virtual machines (VM), to communicate over a simulated network" (p. 1). A benefit of this simulation approach is that network analysis can be performed prior to procuring potentially expensive equipment and spending valuable time deploying it. This tool is helpful for experts who want to train in high-fidelity cyber environments. New cyber capabilities are emerging quickly, and there must exist an efficient evaluation of an environment's security posture. A tool with this capability enables "what-if" experimentation and operational planning and training. Furthermore, the simulated environments should be easy to define, deploy, maintain, and modify.

While running experiments, CyberVAN utilizes the Network Simulator 3 (ns-3) tool, which also consists of the 5G network elements that will design the 5G topology and the new cyber architecture. In Industry, the ns-3 simulator is known as one of the best network simulation tools for 5G applications because of its scalability and open-source availability. Since Peraton Labs designed CyberVAN to use the ns-3 simulator, the researcher excluded ns-3 as an option during the research tool selection process. Because ns-3 is built as a collection of libraries that can be integrated with other libraries, this is feasible. CyberVAN users access the tool via the Internet and use a "scenario-design" graphical user interface (GUI) for network design according to "CyberVAN: Cyber Virtual Assured Network" (Peraton Labs, n.d., p. 2). The source continues and states that the scenario management GUI is used for network design and provides an environment to log into VMs, run various analytics tools, save experiment results, and pause or restart experiments. Regarding data collection, CyberVAN offers a lot of capabilities in this area, including packet captures (PCAPs), network flow records, log files, and a user activity tracker tool that tracks human-to-computer interactions such as keystroke events and shell commands. The tool can also simulate user activity driving real applications on end hosts, generating realistic network traffic (Peraton Labs, n.d., p. 2). The researcher was intrigued by the capabilities of CyberVAN and designated this network simulation tool as the favorite for conducting the research topic.

NetSim is a leading network emulator that performs modeling and simulation (M&S). It was created by Tetcos and is located in Bangalore, India. It is used by 500+ organizations across 30+ countries. According to Tetcos (n.d.), the emulator can be used for testing application performance subject to network effects, R&D in new protocol design and testing your protocol performance with real applications, design state testing before the actual hardware/software capability is ready, and integration into cyber test beds. TrustRadius (n.d.) in "NetSim Reviews & Ratings" also mentions that NetSim is a simulation environment that caters to many industries, from commercial telecommunications to the DoD, and enables users to examine how new devices and protocols behave in a virtual network.

The tool's capabilities listed above substantiate NetSim as a system with great scalability but a steep learning curve due to the many features and options. Additionally,

NetSim is one of the best options for performing M&S for the 5G standard. However, the NetSim Standard service is not a free or inexpensive software option. The single-user license for NetSim's 5G Library costs $4637 for the perpetual license and $2087 for an annual license. There is a NetSim Academic version; however, it does not include the 5G library. The researcher inquired for more information from Tetcos Support about the pricing for both versions, but they did not disclose the cost for the Academic version.

Support stated that this version was significantly cheaper than the Standard service cost. Unfortunately, NetSim Academic is not beneficial since the 5G library is not offered for this version. The researcher decided that NetSim would not be the ideal option due its high cost.

Chang (1999) in "Network Simulations with OPNET" states, "OPNET (Optimized Network Engineering Tool) provides a comprehensive development environment for the specification, simulation, and performance analysis of communication networks. A large range of communication systems, from a single LAN to global satellite networks, can be supported, and discrete event simulations are used as the means of analyzing system performance and behavior" (p. 308). OPNET provides three models, also called domains, to develop system illustrations. The three OPNET Models are the Network, Node, and Process Domains. Each of these models will be explained in the following few paragraphs.

The Network Model consists of the actual topology of the communications network interconnecting its entities, nodes or links. Node capabilities are realized and defined in the Node Model, but subnetworks add to the complexity of this particular model. For the Node Model, Chang (1999) specifies, “Communication devices created and interconnected at the network level need to be specified in the node domain using the Node Editor” (p. 309). Each node in this model is a block structure where its functionality is defined by the underlying model, which is the Process Model. This model designates the behavior and logic flow of the programmable modules by utilizing a statetransition diagram approach specifying protocol types, applications, or queueing policy. In response to events, states will graphically showcase the progression of a process. One process can generate new processes, referred to as child processes, to address sub-tasks, which is thus called the parent process.

The initial intent of this Praxis was to determine which OPNET model would be the most efficient in deriving the new 5G cyber architecture. However, Reuters (2012) announced that Riverbed Technology Inc. bought OPNET for about $1 billion to gain a competitive advantage over the other networking gear makers (para. 1). Riverbed combined OPNET’s capabilities with its network monitoring product to deliver an enhanced product. After thoroughly researching the new Riverbed Modeler, the researcher determined that it would not serve as the ideal network simulation tool for this Praxis.

Like CyberVAN, Riverbed Modeler provides a developmental environment that serves well in research and development (R&D) applications to model and analyze communication networks. Riverbed Modeler enables you to optimize investment by testing and demonstrating technology designs before production. This modeler incorporates the features and capabilities after OPNET merged with the Riverbed product, so the software satisfies the network type consideration and scalability requirements. Additionally, Riverbed Modeler provides intuitive visualization capabilities to display simulation results and analyze network behavior effectively. In terms of cost, Riverbed did not publicly disclose the licensing cost for the software. The researcher contacted the sales and support team; however, the group was unresponsive and did not answer whether the modeler is a free and open-source product.

2.7 Use Case Selection

When creating a cyber architecture, selecting a use case is part of the design process. This step is necessary because it scopes the architecture design into a practical, real-life scenario, which helps to substantiate the purpose of designing the architecture. The author could consider possible use cases, including healthcare, manufacturing, federal government, logistics, smart cities, etc. The researcher considered several use cases that could be used where an architectural need is necessary to enhance the security of data assets in a real-life scenario. Axonius (n.d.) adds more context by stating, "An essential component of a security program is defining security use cases and building solutions around them, and a security use case is an attack scenario that a security control, policy, or guideline is intended to prevent or mitigate" (para. 1). Focusing the methodology in designing the architecture to a use case will help answer the researcher's questions regarding the design's key performance parameters (KPPs), yielding conclusions about the architecture's efficacy. The organizational profile that includes the types of data assets within a particular industry will look different for distinct businesses. Capturing the existing and missing capabilities of a system within a specific sector is possible when applying a use case to a research topic.

Moreover, the design process of a cybersecurity architecture will differ depending on the industry. For example, the complexity of the architecture differs in the number of user equipment devices between a smart city within a municipality and the production of goods in a manufacturing warehouse. Cost, complexity, and network performance are practical values to evaluate when designing a cybersecurity architecture, and they have proportional relationships. In other words, the cost for the architecture design and implementation is higher if the complexity and security of the system is greater. The tradeoff details of each architecture are evaluated in Chapter 3.

2.8 Conclusion

In conclusion, the literature review was divided into ten elements: Introduction, Literature Searches, Articles, Federal Publications, Journals, 5G Overview, Perimeter Security Strategy, Zero Trust Strategy, Network Simulation, Use Case Selection, and Conclusion. Several federal publications, journals, articles, and other literature searches were cited by the researcher to substantiate the importance of securing 5G communications. Furthermore, the 5G Overview and Zero Trust Strategy details the 5G mobile network, its importance to the critical infrastructure, and the background of the PS strategy, which has been a traditional security practice in the cybersecurity field for many decades.

The ZT strategy, a new approach in securing critical assets, is a deperimeterization effort in which every asset within an organization's network is not trusted. Chapter 3 explains the methodology used to develop the new cyber architecture for secure 5G communications.

Chapter 3—Methodology

3.1 Introduction

In this section, the methodology in evaluating the research questions and testing the research hypotheses will be examined. Again, there currently is not a standard that facilitates an efficient cyber architecture that secures the 5G mobile network, which prompted the author to perform this work. IEEE (n.d.) defines architecture as "The fundamental organization of a system in its environment embodied in its components, their relationships to each other, and the principles guiding its design and evolution" (para. 16). The researcher will represent the architecture as a network diagram simulated in CyberVAN.

Before simulating the cyber architecture, the attack surface of the 5G mobile network must be captured. The scope of work focuses on securing the IoT devices utilized by the public in the UE network segment. The researcher believed this was the best approach in completing the Praxis due to the interest of time. Objectives are defined before performing the implementation tasks for validation purposes, so this step will initiate the research's methodology. The researcher must also examine the vulnerabilities and threats that could exploit the 5G mobile network before evaluating the most applicable use case and dataset for this research. Risk management frameworks are compared to help in selecting an applicable process that is effective in executing continuous monitoring and improvement for the architecture. Lastly, the development of a security architecture policy needs to be enforced, so the author will provide input in composing a post-deployment policy of 5G security. The final product will be a successful CyberVAN simulation of the 5G mobile network scenario, demonstrating an efficient balance between cost, complexity, and network performance. Limited simulation examples of ZT microsegmentation encapsulate the author's scope of work. Therefore, this methodology will incorporate the microsegmentation technique referenced in NIST Special Publication (SP) 800-207. The process map that illustrates every subsequent phase from start to finish is as follows:

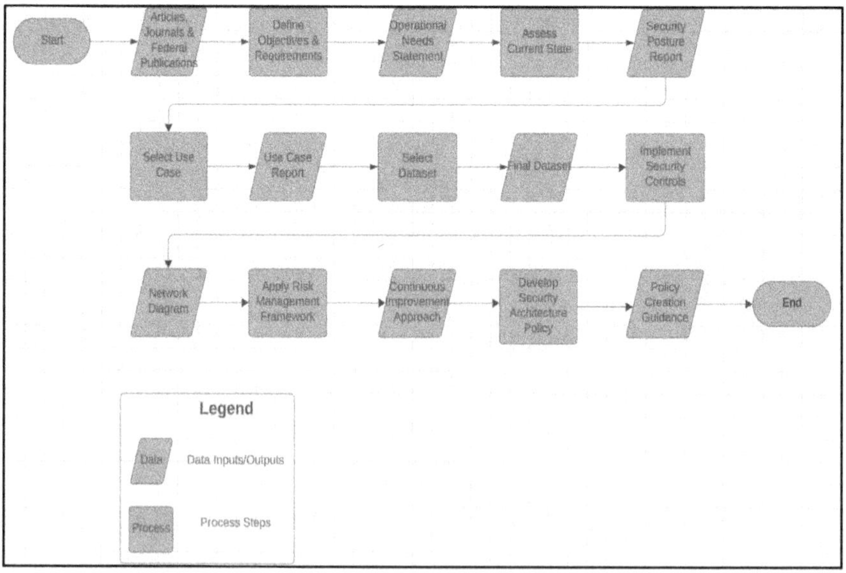

Figure 4. Methodology Process Map.

The legend in Figure 4 designates the blue square blocks as the process steps, and the pink parallelogram blocks are the data inputs and outputs.

The research articles, journals, and federal publications cited in this Praxis document the technical gaps in a secure 5G mobile network architecture and feed into the Define Objectives & Requirements process step. An Operational Needs Statement (ONS) is the product of this process after reviewing documents and completing the objectives. The ONS is the input into the Assess Current State process that evaluates today's security posture of the 5G mobile network, which then yields the Security Posture Report that describes the dire need for the security architecture. The following process step (Select Use Case) is essential in constructing an architecture because it provides context on how the architecture can enhance the security posture of a real-life application. The Use Case Report will include the several use cases that the researcher considered before selecting the ideal application for this research. For the Select Dataset process, a few datasets will be evaluated by the researcher and then select the best one to serve as the input into the architecture for testing purposes for the CyberVAN simulation. Next, the Implement Security Controls process step will elaborate on the necessary network elements and the design process of the architectures. This step will yield the component specifications and network diagram and then feed into the Select Risk Management Framework process. A security framework for the 5G mobile network will be recommended for the selected use by process completion after evaluating several options. The product of this process is the final approach of the continuous monitoring and improvement activity. Lastly, the Develop Security Architecture Policy step will detail the current position of the 5G security policy and recommendations on what federal and commercial organizations must enact as policy in order to ensure cyber protection of the 5G mobile network. This process step yields the risk management recommendations during the maintenance stage, which leads to the restart of the entire process map. Risks change over time due to new discoveries of vulnerabilities or revisions of objectives and requirements. Therefore, the Define Objectives & Requirements, Apply Risk Management Framework, and Develop Security Architecture Policy process steps work in tandem to address cyber protection against new threats and account for necessary changes to the cyber resilience strategy.

As mentioned before in Chapter 1, below are the research questions (RQs) and hypotheses (H) that the author will test and substantiate:

RQ1: Which network topology (User Equipment-Radio Network Access, User

Equipment-New Radio) in CyberVAN is most effective in completing the scope of work?

RQ2: Can CyberVAN enhance the security resilience of the 5G architecture?

RQ3: Does the Perimeter Security, Zero Trust Microsegmentation, or Non-

Standalone Model perform better in network latency?

H1: The 5G User Equipment-New Radio topology in CyberVAN is most effective in completing the scope of work.

H2: CyberVAN will enhance the security resilience of the 5G architecture.

H3: The Perimeter Security performs better in network latency.

3.2 Define Objectives & Requirements

Before defining the objectives for this Praxis, it is important to reiterate the scope of work of this project. Again, the scope of work (SoW) is to develop and simulate a security architecture for the 5G mobile network through Modeling & Simulation (M&S) and data analytics to identify risks and establish appropriate mitigations so that untrusted technology currently implemented in the 5G network is secured. The researcher will explore several architecture design options and select one to secure the 5G mobile network use case. There is a close relationship between requirements and architecture; however, the questions they answer and their outputs to help conclude the research work differ. Below are the restated research objectives mentioned in Section 1.5:

- Evaluate the security profile of different 5G architecture models in the Cyber

  Virtual Assured Network (CyberVAN) simulator
- Assess the network latency results of each 5G architecture designed in CyberVAN and leverage statistical analysis to magnify the differences in the outcomes

The researcher will design three models and compare their security posture differences and network latency results. Therefore, the functional requirements of this research are as follows:

- An architecture must enforce Perimeter Security by implementing the Traditional Model
- An architecture must enforce Zero Trust by implementing the microsegmentation technique per NIST Special Publication 800-207

The author will present the results in Chapter 4 and recommend the best architectural solution after outcome analysis. Every step of the process map that was demonstrated in Section 3.1 will be executed and thoroughly explained. The objectives and requirements will be exhibited in Chapter 4 where the results of the two architecture models are displayed.

3.3 Assess Current State

Now that the objectives are defined, the researcher will assess the current state of the 5G mobile network's security posture. Currently, there is not a post-deployment security standard for the 5G mobile network. The CISA 5G Strategy was released in 2020 when 5G was initially deployed; however, there are not any research projects exhibiting a new architecture for the 5G mobile network in a simulated environment such as CyberVAN that is scoped to secure Internet of Things (IoT) devices in the UE segment of the network. The conversation of secure-by-design just began to ramp up when the 6G discussion initiated not long ago but did not initiate before 5G was deployed. Because the secure-by-design approach was not implemented for the 5G mobile network, the number of exploitable vulnerabilities before they are introduced on the market will not be reduced at the same magnitude otherwise. Quality management concerns about the cost of early design defects could not be addressed since there is not an architectural standard for securing 5G communications. The findings of this section will influence the design of the architecture models that the author constructs.

3.4 Select Use Case

The 5G mobile network can serve many different applications in Industry so that business operations are executed more efficiently. There are two industries in 5G that can quickly improve operational efficiency: healthcare and manufacturing. In healthcare, Internet of Things (IoT) devices are used to construct an internal network to track subsystems such as ventilators, insulin pumps, electrocardiogram (EKG) machines, etc. Additionally, leveraging 5G would help managers know the inventory levels for equipment and what systems need repair. The use case for 5G in the manufacturing industry is also known as Industrial IoT (IIOT) and was one of the first industries to reap the benefits of more operational efficiency after 5G deployment. 5G enables increased network capacity and low latency requirements to support IIoT devices and robotic machines in complex manufacturing environments. Smart cities are considered a concept of the future but are being implemented today. This use case is a great option to showcase how beneficial the 5G mobile network has been for city governments in regard to public utility tracking, waste management, water treatment, and city infrastructure monitoring. However, the researcher deemed this use case too complex for this Praxis due to the interest of time. The smart city uses case warrants a longer timeline for conducting research. The author selected the manufacturing and healthcare industries as the top two use case options because of scalability. Both industries include examples that can be easily scaled down into a manageable network size that will be constructed in

CyberVAN. In 2023, the Department of Health and Human Services (HHS) declared, “The healthcare sector is particularly vulnerable to cybersecurity risks, and the stakes for patient care and safety are exceptionally high” (p. 1). Moreover, the sector is an attractive target for threat actors due to technological dependence and sensitive data, such as Protected Health Information (PHI) and Payment Card Industry (PCI) data. The HHS motivated the researcher to select healthcare as the industry use case since there is not much cybersecurity research to focus on securing IoT equipment in the medical environment.

3.5 Select Datasets

The researcher conducted extensive research to locate attack data for the

CyberVAN simulation. The sources were found by searching on Google and the George Washington University (GWU) Gelman Online Library. One of the collected datasets will serve as an input to the security architecture for security control testing. The primary concern regarding the security of the 5G mobile network is the UE network segment since massive Internet of Things (mIoT) and other types of user devices are concentrated on this side of the mobile network. In this case, the healthcare network utilizes remote patient monitoring systems to record patients’ attributes and vital signs, Wireless Fidelity (Wi-Fi) connections within the facilities to connect sensors, video-recording systems to perform behavioral recognition, etc. The weakest link in cybersecurity is the human factor due to users' ignorance and carelessness, so the UE network must be secured using the appropriate security controls for the simulated scenario to prevent lateral movement by adversaries. Furthermore, the data collection effort will yield necessary revisions of federal and commercial 5G security publications. Once the author determined that it was optimal to concentrate on user equipment security, the researcher shifted focus to the appropriate data that would serve as the ideal data source to yield the desired outcomes.

The attack data sources initially found by the author are as follows:

#	Name	Source	Description	Format	Release Year	# of Records
1	Edge-IIOTSet	IEEE DataPort	The IoT data are generated from various IoT devices and can identify and analyze fourteen IoT and IIoT connectivity attacks	.csv	2023	1176
2	ECUIoHT	Australia Edith Cowan University	ECU-IoHT is a dataset that was developed consisting of different attacks performed that exploit various vulnerabilities.	.xlsx	2020	5000

3	IoT-23 Dataset	Google Sites (IoT Dataset Search)	The IoT-23 Dataset was created consisting of 10 different attacks to exploit several vulnerabilities.	.csv	2022	3500

Table 3. Attack Datasets and their Descriptions.

The attack types are primarily brute force such as botnets, denial-of-service (DoS), and DDoS attacks.

The researcher originally considered the Edge-IIoTSet before healthcare was selected as the business use case for this research. The researcher's initial thought when locating this dataset was to utilize it for a manufacturing use case and demonstrate the implemented security controls for the UE network within a warehouse facility. The controls would have facilitated additional security for the integrated sensors operating to enhance production. For example, programmable logic controllers (PLCs) are a key part of IIoT and are used for industrial automation. They are known to control analog or digital sensors and communicate through various types of complex interfaces in the food, plastic, steel, pharmaceutical, and automotive industries. However, the Industrial Internet of Things (IIoT) is also used in healthcare for monitoring the performance of subsystems such as monitoring sensors and other user devices. The Australia Edith Cowan University Internet of Healthcare Things (ECU-IoHT) was a dataset specifically designed for a healthcare use case such as this research. According to Australia Edith Cowan University (2020), there aren't enough datasets that demonstrate cyber vulnerabilities in healthcare (para. 3). Therefore, the University created a dataset reflecting different cyberattacks on the Internet of Healthcare Things (IoHT). The author added this dataset to the list of options since the healthcare domain was one of the top two business use cases. IoT-23 was found on Google Sites under Internet of Things (IoT) Dataset Search. IoT-23 was a generic IoT dataset suited for the researcher's use case. However, the first two options were deemed better for this research due to the Praxis' scope of work. However, it is essential to note that the ECU-IoHT dataset is already formatted and prepared for the architecture, so data imputation is not required. Section 3.4 designates the healthcare sector as the selected business use case; therefore, the author believes that the ECU-IoHT dataset is the most applicable option for the use case. The packet capture data encompassed in the dataset are time, source IP address, destination IP address, protocol type, packet length, packet information, and attack type. For the selected use case, the researcher will select the data designated as an attack, such as Address Resolution Protocol (ARP) spoofing. According to Lenaerts-Bergmans (2022), "ARP spoofing or ARP poisoning is a form of spoofing attack used to intercept data. A hacker commits an ARP spoofing attack by tricking one device into sending messages to the hacker instead of the intended recipient" (para. 1). The ECU-IoHT dataset will yield the outputs of the simulated models that will be compared in Chapter 4.

3.6 Implement Security Controls

The key components of the architecture designs will pertain to the UE-RAN, UE-NR, and NSA applications. Moreover, two different architecture designs will exhibit the PS and ZT microsegmentation strategies after the author substantiates the optimal topology between UE-RAN and UE-NR. For example, PS will include only one firewall to defend the network boundary by monitoring traffic incoming from the Internet. However, the ZT Microsegmentation Model consists of a firewall at several nodes since implicit trust does not exist in the Zero Trust Architecture. The component types and the number of security devices necessary to complete the design will differ between both designs.

The researcher will describe key components necessary for the 5G models. The inventory assets for both models are as follows:

- Radio Access Network subsystem - gNB (Next Generation Node B)
- User Equipment Network subsystems - VM host machines, firewalls, routers, hubs, switches
- Core Network subsystems - MME, SGW, PGW, VM host machines, firewalls, routers, hubs, switches

For the UE network, it may include router(s), firewall(s), hub(s), switch(es), and virtual machines (VMs) representing user or Internet of Things (IoT) devices. The Radio Access Network (RAN) only includes either an Evolved Node B (eNB) base station, which is utilized for 4G LTE, or the Next Generation Node B (gNB) base station that is deployed for mediating communications between the 5G New Radio (NR) devices and the CN. The CN will consist of 4G LTE CN elements, which constructs the EPC enabling the operation of 5G New Radio (NR). These elements include the MME, PGW, and SGW. The MME is the key component of the CN and is considered the control node managing the mobility of user devices. It ensures that the user devices remain connected to the network without interruption. The PGW is the gateway between the UE network and external data packet networks and manages Internet Protocol (IP) addresses for UE devices connected to the 5G mobile network. The SGW is deemed the local mobility anchor that forwards and routes packets to and from the gNB base station and PGW. The communications between the gNB base station and MME are considered the control plane since the functions performed by these elements involve session management, which is outside of the user's control. However, the user plane consists of the gNB base station, SGW, and PGW elements before the user is connected to the Internet.

Architecture models will be designed and compared to evaluate the optimal solution for the use case. One architecture is the Traditional Model, also known as the PS Model, where a cyber defense mechanism such as a firewall defends the perimeter of the subject network. In this case, a firewall will be used to defend the perimeter of the UE network. The firewall will allow authorized traffic and block unauthorized users from accessing the healthcare facility's internal network. The firewalls must be configured to perform as expected so that adversaries cannot compromise the sensitive data stored within the UE network. The healthcare network must be compliant to the Health

Insurance Portability and Accountability Act (HIPAA). CDC (n.d.) states, “The Health Insurance Portability and Accountability Act (HIPAA) of 1996 establishes federal standards protecting sensitive health information from disclosure without patient's consent” (para. 1). It was enacted into law on August 21, 1996, by the U.S. Congress.

Another architecture is the ZT Model, which eliminates implicit trust. There are several techniques to enforce this strategy, but the author will design the ZT

Microsegmentation Model. In this scenario, a firewall will be assigned to defend every user device within the UE network instead of one cyber defense mechanism protecting the network boundary. The comparison of these models will help substantiate the three hypotheses. The differences between the PS and ZT Microsegmentation Models are shown below:

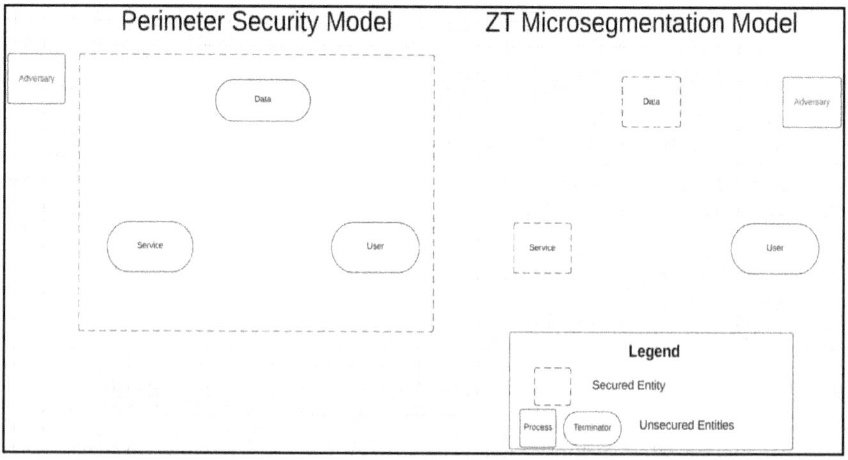

Figure 5. Perimeter Security Model vs. Zero Trust Model (adapted from Sahlin,

2023, p. 6).

The ZT Microsegmentation Model, as demonstrated in Figure 5, will help substantiate the ideal architecture solution for the healthcare use case. The dotted squares denote the defended boundary of the internal network in the PS Model or the secured data and service entity in Figure 5.

The CyberVAN simulator was elected as the Praxis research tool to design the 5G architectures. The reasons for the selection of this simulator were delineated in Chapter 2, Section 2.6 (Network Simulation) of this Praxis. The security controls selected to secure the architecture and substantiate the hypotheses will depend on the model. These security controls are showcased in the results in Chapter 4 and help select the ideal architectural solution for the healthcare industry.

3.7 Apply Risk Management Framework

Continuous monitoring and improvement are an ongoing cycle to enhance the security of the subject system. In this case, the recommended architectural solution, which will provide balance between cost, complexity, and network performance, requires a continual improvement process to enhance the system's security profile. Additionally, the architecture design will need to be reconstructed if any changes to the UE network occur, such as the expansion of user devices or adjustments to the security controls. The UE network expansion is necessary for evaluating the security of users and Internet of Things (IoT) devices for the 5G SA model. This is future work for other researchers, which will be further explained in Chapter 5. The researcher will evaluate frameworks created by NIST and MITRE to apply to the selected use case specifically. Ultimately, the researcher will deem the ideal risk management process for continuous monitoring and improvement.

Several cybersecurity frameworks currently exist to guide Industry on how to defend an organization's critical data assets. The researcher acknowledges that both NIST and MITRE Corporation created frameworks that commercial businesses and government agencies use to mitigate risk of data exfiltration. NIST released the first iteration of the Cybersecurity Framework (CSF) in 2014; however, CSF 2.0 was recently released to the public in February 2024. CSF Tools (2024) states, "The Cybersecurity Framework (CSF) 2.0 is designed to help organizations of all sizes and sectors — including industry, government, academia, and nonprofit — to manage and reduce their cybersecurity risks" (para. 1). NIST CSF 2.0 was designed to help organizations of all sizes and business sectors to manage cybersecurity risk. This framework tailors itself to a specific use case, which is a major advantage over the two MITRE frameworks. According to MITRE (n.d.), "MITRE Adversarial Tactics, Techniques, and Common Knowledge (ATT&CK) is a knowledge base of adversarial tactics, techniques, and procedures (TTPs) based on real-life observations" (para. 1). It is an open framework for any person or organization to use at no cost. Detection, Denial, and Disruption Framework Empowering Network Defense (D3FEND) is the complementary framework to MITRE ATT&CK that focuses on the defensive techniques of an organization. The National

Security Agency (NSA) funded the development of this knowledge base to improve the cybersecurity of the DoD. It is still a growing collection of defensive tactics, techniques, and procedures (TTPs) designed to neutralize cyberattacks from adversaries. The MITRE frameworks are globally used within the cybersecurity community by the Federal Government and Industry seeking to gain an understanding of adversarial attacks and defensive strategies. However, the researcher decided that neither of these frameworks were ideal since they provide general guidance but not procedures that are specific and relevant to an organization's use case. Therefore, the CSF 2.0 framework was identified and selected as the ideal option for this use case.

CSF 2.0 consists of a process for building cybersecurity profiles. NIST (2024) in "NIST Cybersecurity Framework 2.0: Quick-Start Guide for Creating and Using Organizational Profiles" states, "An Organizational Profile describes an organization's current and/or target cybersecurity posture in terms of cybersecurity outcomes from the Cybersecurity Framework (CSF) Core. Organizational Profiles are used to understand, tailor, assess, and prioritize cybersecurity outcomes based on an organization's mission objectives, stakeholder expectations, threat landscape, and requirements" (p. 1). These Profiles can evaluate how well desired results are attained. An Organizational Profile can be categorized into a Current or Target Profile. An organization's Current Profile outlines the results it is now attaining and how each is being accomplished. However, a Target

Profile details the desired CSF outcomes that an organization has prioritized to achieve its cybersecurity objectives. Furthermore, it takes potential changes to the organization's security posture into consideration, which may include new technology adoption, revised requirements, and threat intelligence trends. The CSF five-step process compares the desired Target Profile to the assessed Current Profile before performing the gap analysis, which yields an action plan that details how to progress from the current to the desired state. The Organizational Profile creation process is as follows:

1. Scope the Organizational Profile
2. Gather Needed Information
3. Create the Organizational Profile
4. Analyze Gaps and Create an Action Plan
5. Implement Action Plan and Update Profile

The first step is to Scope the Organizational Profile. It is important to note that an organization can possess more than one profile depending on several factors. These factors may include the technology category, data types, users, etc. In the healthcare use case, three Organizational Profiles can be defined since they are scoped into three distinct categories. The technology category for the use case would be Information Technology (IT) since resources such as e-mail systems, enterprise resource planning (ERP), and data analytics are utilized in daily operations. IT aligns with the Organizational Profile since it focuses on the processing, transmission, storage, and management of data. In regard to data types, healthcare is one of the few industries that possesses more than two data types. This business use case possesses Personally Identifiable Information (PII), Protected Health Information (PHI), and Payment Card Industry (PCI) data. PII examples include Social Security Number (SSN), Driver's License Number, and Passport Number, whereas PHI includes insurance information, billing information, dates of service, details of service, and provider and patient correspondence. PCI includes some of the PII information noted above in addition to Credit Card Chip PIN, Credit Card Number, and Permanent Account Number (PAN). The Payment Card Industry Data Security Standard (PCI DSS) governs debit and credit card transactions for the healthcare sector. It is imperative for healthcare entities to sustain a secure network by implementing strong security controls and continuously monitor security performance by enabling a feedback loop between the maintenance and planning stages of the security architecture. Lastly, the healthcare industry has two user types: healthcare provider employees and patients.

The second step of the CSF process is to Gather Needed Information. Common sources of information for this step include Community Profiles and the NIST Organizational Profile Template. According to NIST (2024), "A Community Profile is a baseline of CSF outcomes created and published to address shared interests and goals among a number of organizations. A Community Profile is typically intended for a particular sector or subsector, technology, threat type, or other use case." The holistic healthcare sector could serve as a Community Profile since it encompasses many medical facilities that share interests and goals. However, it is very difficult to capture an overarching risk management process for this Community Profile without understanding the unique challenges of each individual Organizational Profile in detail. The CSF Organizational Profile Template is available to the public on the NIST website to complete, but it is very comprehensive and would take an extensive amount of time to finish. However, the template is located on the NIST CSF 2.0 website. The third step of the CSF process is Create the Organizational Profile. For step 3, the healthcare organization defines the desired CSF outcomes, the Current Profile's practices, and the Target Profile's priorities and goals. The gaps between each profile are where step 4 comes into play to establish a plan to transition from the Current and Target Profiles. The fourth step is Analyze Gaps & Create an Action Plan. Once the profile is completed, the organization will be able to examine how the Current and Target Profiles differ from one another. These differences found are called "gaps" and are yielded from the comparative analysis between current and best practices across people, processes, and technology. The conclusions made about the gaps are then established as candidate improvements. Action plans should exhibit the current practices of architecture (people, process, technology) and target goals, including outcome descriptions, implementation examples, and references such as NIST SP 800-30 and 800-37. Additionally, the action plan outlines the program's enhancements, and it is important to consider the risks, possibilities, and available financial and human resources.

The CSF references tools, controls, and implementation resources to facilitate gap analysis and action plan development. NIST advises using the Reference Tool to adhere to links related to NIST SP 800-53 security controls from pertinent Target Profile subcategories. Informative references help determine how to accomplish CSF outcomes. This is a best practice to use when executing this step and implementation examples are ideal for implementing best practices. Implementation examples are just descriptive ways of how CSF outcomes can be achieved. They do not have to be a comprehensive list of all actions. The examples are beneficial in helping the organization to think about concrete steps in achieving the outcomes.

The last step of the process is Implement Action Plan & Update Profile. NIST (2024) in "NIST Cybersecurity Framework 2.0: Quick-Start Guide for Creating and

Using Organizational Profiles" states the following about implementing an action plan, "The Action Plan is fulfilled through any combination of management, programmatic, and technical controls. As those controls are implemented, the Organizational Profile can be used to track implementation status" (p. 8). Security controls and associated risks can be monitored through Key Performance Indicators (KPIs) and Key Risk Indicators (KRIs) can be used to track security controls and related hazards (NIST, 2024, p. 8). NIST SP 800-37 further elaborates on KPI, KRI, and Risk Tolerance. Action plan activities are imperative in the continuous improvement and cyber risk management process. NIST SP 800-30 explains risk assessments, which can be conducted through KPI and KRI evaluation or by using risk tolerance statements that illustrate the probability and impact of risks. Modifications to risks, likelihoods, and impacts could influence updates to the Organizational Profile. Lastly, Chapter 4 will reference the selected risk management framework and add a few more details on how the healthcare industry should apply it.

3.8 Develop Security Architecture Policy

In this section, the researcher will develop the layout of the 5G Security Policy for Healthcare Corporations. This use case will be more applicable if the policy is enacted for one corporation. A healthcare corporation includes Johns Hopkins Health System (JHHS), MedStar Health, etc. It is imperative to enact an architectural cyber protection policy because there currently is not a cybersecurity policy specifically focused on the implementation of architecture as a whole. Again, cyber architecture consists of people, processes, and technology. Typically, security controls configured to defend critical data assets are only considered on the technological side of the architecture and not in other focus areas. President Joe Biden, in the 2023 National Cybersecurity Strategy released on March 1, 2023, initially presented the United States (U.S.) Government's approach towards securing the digital infrastructure by using Federal incentives to facilitate security building and ensuring accountability of data stewards (The White House, 2023,

p. 19). HHS released the "Healthcare Sector Cybersecurity Strategy" in 2023; however, there was minimal information on how to implement a redundant cybersecurity architecture. The document mentions the current cybersecurity activities, such as telehealth guidance enforcement, training offerings, and resource publishing. However, it does not address the sector's cybersecurity architecture and the vision moving forward in this matter. Therefore, it is in the healthcare sector's best interest to fulfill the President's vision of securing its systems and protecting patients from cyber threats. In order to accomplish this objective, recommendations on the vision and architectural solution for the sector must be established by the policy. The researcher will introduce how to develop the cyber architectural policy for a healthcare corporation that encompasses a more holistic approach to securing the 5G use case.

The researcher will establish the following sections in the HHS strategy of the ultimate architectural solution: Executive Summary, Introduction, Strategic Goals & Objectives, HHS Zero Trust Approach, and Conclusion. The "DoD Zero Trust Strategy" composed by the DoD CIO in 2022 was used as a template for the healthcare sector's architectural strategy. The Executive Summary will detail the "Five Years into the Future" strategy for the researcher's architectural solution and include the information such as the problem statement and current state assessment that were designated in Chapters 1 and 3, respectively (DoD CIO, 2022, p. 4). The introduction will provide an overview of the purpose of the policy for a healthcare corporation. Strategic Goals & Objectives section is where the long-term goals are defined in deploying the recommended architectural solution and how the short-term objectives are accomplished to realize the strategy's vision (DoD CIO, 2022, p. 1). The HHS Zero Trust Approach elaborates on the methodology for accelerating the adoption of the suggested architectural solution (DoD CIO, 2022, p. 7). Moreover, assumptions must be made in the beginning to guide the execution of the strategy. The Conclusion section will end the strategy by reiterating the vision towards securing the healthcare sector from an architectural standpoint and how realistic it is for Industry to accomplish this strategic goal. The recommended architectural solution following the comparison of the Perimeter Security and Zero Trust Microsegmentation Models in the next chapter will serve as the resolution to the problem specified in the scope of work (SoW). After the results of the hypotheses are showcased in Chapter 4, the researcher will present the strategy's title and the content for each section in Chapter 5.

3.9 Conclusion

In conclusion, the researcher delineated the Introduction, Define Objectives & Requirements, Assess Current State, Select Use Case, Select Dataset, Implement Security Controls, Apply Risk Management Framework, and Develop Security Architecture Policy processes performed to substantiate the Praxis. The author created the process map in this subsequent order because the objectives and requirements of the architecture must be established prior to selecting an applicable use case and dataset for the research. These process steps executed the planning phase of the Kelley and Moyle model before jumpstarting the design stage by completing the Implement Security Controls process. Additionally, the continuous improvement cycle is necessary to monitor the security performance of the architecture and enable a feedback loop between the implementation and maintenance phases back to the initial planning process to introduce new changes to the objectives and requirements. The Apply Risk Management Framework process step addresses these concerns for a continuous monitoring and improvement cycle and applies it to the healthcare use case after the security controls are implemented. Lastly, the Develop Security Architecture Policy step introduces a cybersecurity architecture policy for the healthcare sector that recommends architectural solutions given the constraints of a particular corporation. In Chapter 4, the researcher will present and explain the results after executing every process step.

Chapter 4—Results

4.1 Introduction

In this Chapter, the methodology results will be illustrated and explained in detail. The architecture was successfully designed and meets all the objectives and requirements mentioned in Section 3.2. Furthermore, the substantiation of the hypotheses declared in Chapter 1 and Section 3.1 will be demonstrated in this Chapter as well. For Hypothesis 1 (H1) and Hypothesis 2 (H2), qualitative assessments were made to support the claims that the 5G NSA model was the most time-efficient basis in constructing the rest of the cyber architecture (H1) and that a simulation-based security architecture will enhance the security resilience of the 5G network (H2). For Hypothesis 3 (H3), the researcher performed a mix of qualitative and quantitative assessments. The Perimeter Security and Zero Trust Microsegmentation Models were compared, and three values were assessed to facilitate the decision in selecting the most efficient model. These three values are cost, complexity, and network performance. More specifically, the cost and complexity values were assessed qualitatively, and security was evaluated quantitatively.

4.2 Hypothesis 1 Results

Hypothesis 1 (H1), as mentioned in Chapters 1 and 3, reads as follows: "The 5G User Equipment-New Radio topology in CyberVAN is most effective in completing the scope of work." Several 5G models were designed before completing the ideal 5G architecture in CyberVAN because the researcher had to identify the best way to deploy the 5G NR capabilities in the architecture. The author provides context to why a model was not optimal for completing the scope of work.

The researcher compared two different 5G models with distinct security approaches. The initial design is known as the Perimeter Security Model. The first Perimeter Security Model designed in CyberVAN is as follows:

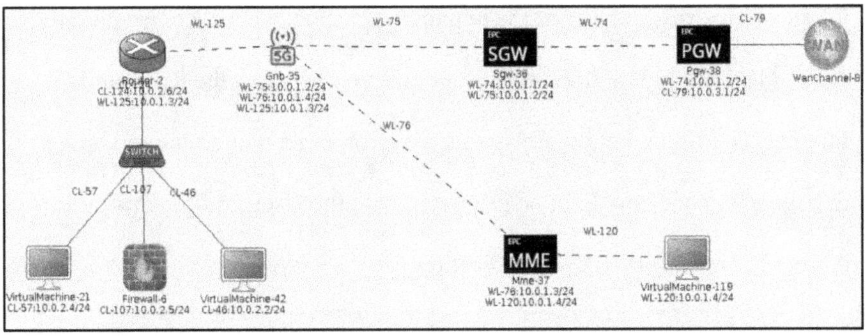

Figure 6. The First Perimeter Security Model Design in CyberVAN. All devices configured to the left of the Next Generation Node B, which is this architecture's Radio Access Network base station, construct the UE network segment. The Evolved Packet Core's network elements, which are the SGW, PGW, and MME, construct the backhaul and core network, enabling connections between the UE, internal systems, and external networks. Wireless links are indicated as "WL," and hardwired links are designated as "CL." However, this model is not optimal because it does not utilize the ns-3 simulation channel designed for 5G communications. This topology was created before the researcher discovered the ns-3 simulation capabilities that CyberVAN possesses. CyberVAN depends on ns-3's 5G simulation models to produce results.

Additionally, the lone firewall should serve as the boundary defense and be placed at the internal network's edge, closer to the Internet user. CyberVAN requires the user to connect a firewall only when a hub or switch is included in the model. Therefore, this design is insufficient due to CyberVAN's requirements for implementing cyber defense mechanisms. The additional models designed by the researcher showcase the lone firewall serving as the internal network's defense at the boundary. Lastly, CyberVAN would only allow a hardwired link to establish a connection between the PGW and the Internet. The figure below showcases the error explaining to the researcher that the ns-3 code could not be generated with the User Equipment-Radio Access Network (UE-RAN) application:

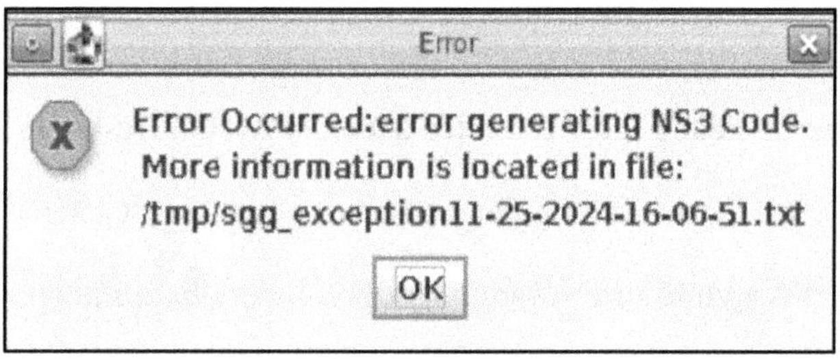

Figure 7. The NS-3 Simulation Code Generation Error in CyberVAN. The first ZT Microsegmentation Model also triggered the above error since it did not include the NR channel in the design.

After completing the Perimeter Security Model, the researcher focused on designing a few models that demonstrate the microsegmentation technique defined in NIST Special Publication 800-207. The first ZT Microsegmentation network diagram of the security architecture in CyberVAN is as follows:

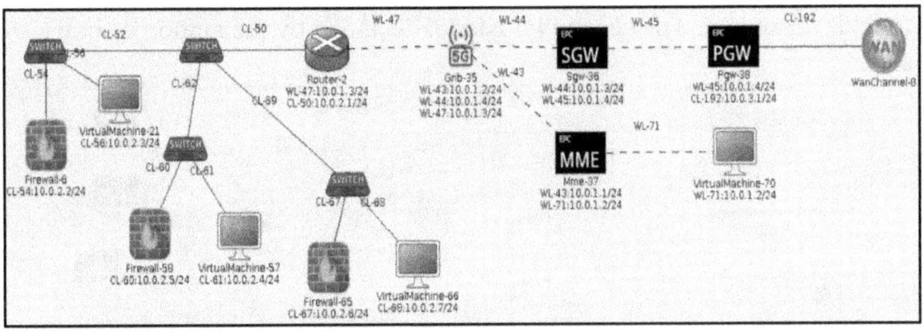

Figure 8. The First Zero Trust Microsegmentation Model Design in CyberVAN. In this model, a simulation firewall was used to microsegment the UE network segment for each IoT device. However, the perimeter firewall issue also applies to this model, so this initial design could be more optimal for simulation use. Furthermore, the author later discovered that simulation firewalls must connect in series and will not apply nextgeneration capability in performing security functions to the switches. The author learned that the ns-3 simulation code for the model performs the packet inspection functionality including additional security devices into the architecture. In turn, the researcher redesigned the Perimeter Security and Zero Trust Microsegmentation Models to properly implement the firewall devices and the core network of the architecture.

After completing the first Perimeter Security Model in CyberVAN, the author discovered that the EPC had to be re-designed to enable greater packet flow between the internal and external networks. The researcher added the backhaul, core, and backbone routers to the second iteration of the Perimeter Security and ZT Microsegmentation Models. The network functions of the enhanced models are described after the second PS

Model is presented. The second PS Model designed by the author is shown below:

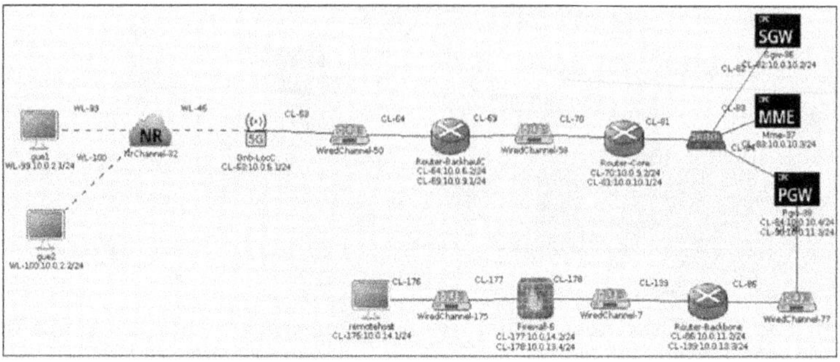

Figure 9. The Second Perimeter Security Model Design in CyberVAN.

This re-designed PS Model consists of three virtual machines (VMs), one Next Generation Node B (gNB), three routers, one perimeter firewall, one switch, and five hubs. The VMs labeled "gue," or next-generation user equipment, represent healthcare user devices at a corporation and wirelessly connect to the 5G New Radio (NR) channel, establishing the UE network segment. The gNB tower is the one Radio Access Network (RAN) element that is responsible for connecting the UE network to the CN for external network access. The switch is essential in bridging the UE network and the Internet through the PGW. CyberVAN requires hubs or switches to connect all other network elements, such as firewalls and routers, so five hubs, or wired channels, were needed to build the PS network diagram. The lone firewall located at the "tail" of the CN was established here to monitor network traffic entering from the Internet VM host named "remotehost". Three routers consist of the PS design and represent the wireless backhaul, core, and backbone. The 5G backhaul, or wireless transport, transfers data from miniaturized base stations called small cells and connects them to the

CN backbone. In turn, the core router connects the 5G Backhaul network to the backbone known as the CN. The backbone router is part of the core network and is responsible for connecting the internal users and the Internet subscriber. The re-designed ZT Microsegmentation Model consists of the same properties explained for the second PS Model; however, the network elements in the design slightly differ. The second ZT Microsegmentation Model is as follows:

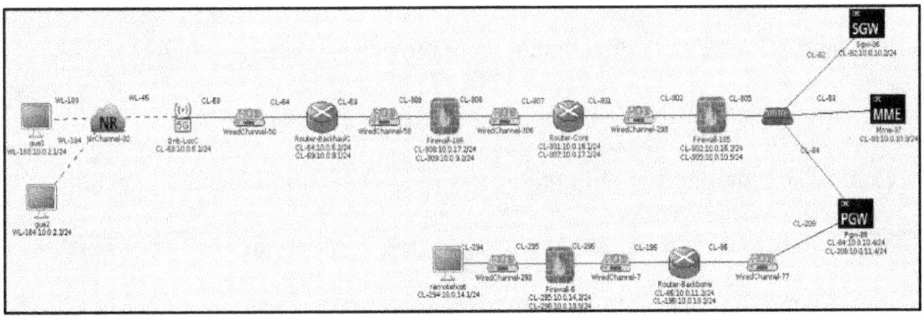

Figure 10. The Second Zero Trust Microsegmentation Model Design in CyberVAN. The design is not much different than the PS Model. The only difference between both models is that the ZT Model consists of three simulation firewalls as opposed to one, as shown in the PS network diagram. Each firewall was configured to protect the router nodes since they are essential to the data forwarding functionality of the CN.

Additionally, they microsegment the architecture so that redundancy is instilled. Redundancy is when there are multiple elements of the same component to ensure that the network can still operate if one component fails. In this case, there is firewall redundancy in the ZT Model since there was only one perimeter firewall defending the boundary in the PS Model.

An alternate architecture was designed in CyberVAN using next-generation routers that includes firewall functionality in filtering network traffic between the UE network and the Internet. The firewall functionality is performed by CyberVAN's 5G simulation models. This NSA model includes the 4G LTE and 5G NR communication planes and implements the User Equipment-New Radio (UE-NR) application. Moreover, Evolved Node B (eNB) nodes represent the RAN networks for the 4G architecture, and

LTE and NR channels were included in the design to generate the UE-NR scenario. The Worldwide Interoperability for Microwave Access (WiMAX) channel, in conjunction with the access point, was implemented to enable higher data speeds for greater coverage areas in the modeling code. This design of the NSA topology is shown below:

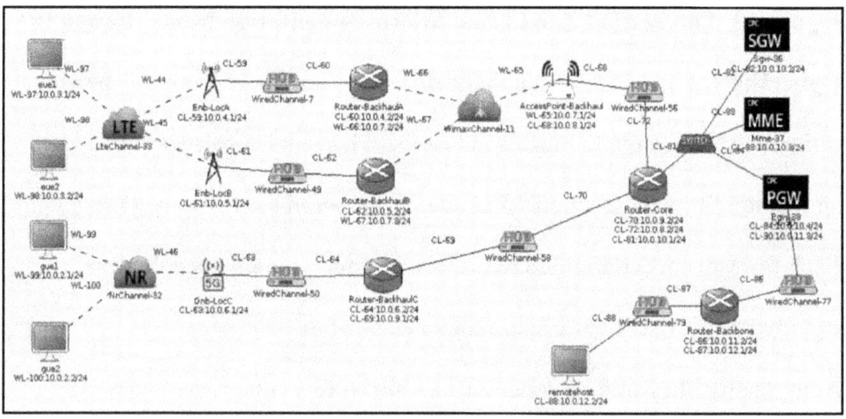

Figure 11. The Non-Standalone Model Design in CyberVAN.

The network latency performance of this model after scenario generation and simulation is presented in Section 4.4. Hypothesis 3 (H3) results of this model will be compared to the other 5G architecture designs illustrated in this section.

The author designed various 5G models to substantiate the UE-RAN or UE-NR as the optimal topology for completing the scope of work. After generating the UE-RAN scenario for the PS and ZT Microsegmentation Models, the researcher determined that building this network diagram for the UE-NR application is optimal for simulation purposes. CyberVAN enables users to design either topology, but the researcher was able to simulate the 5G propagation models and data speeds utilizing the UE-NR system. Furthermore, the UE-RAN topology could not leverage the ns-3 simulation code that CyberVAN uses to run the architecture. After implementing the UE-NR topology, the PS and ZT Microsegmentation Models were successfully generated and simulated. Therefore, the UE-NR topology is the optimal network topology for the researcher to complete the scope of work.

4.3 Hypothesis 2 Results

Hypothesis 2 (H2) reads as follows: "CyberVAN will enhance the security resilience of the 5G mobile network." To substantiate this hypothesis, the researcher elected to conduct this research's work in Cyber Virtual Assured Network (CyberVAN), seeking to explore various ways to enhance the security resilience of the 5GS. Section 4.2 illustrates various architecture designs; however, they come with some constraints. The author selected CyberVAN as the simulator of choice because it is cost-effective and sufficiently capable. However, the primary issue with CyberVAN Version 6.0 is that the author was not able to test the cyber resilience of the architecture models by uploading the selected attack dataset to run the Attack Sequence function. The researcher continuously consulted with Peraton Labs to understand why the function was not operational. The researcher considered other simulators for use; however, the other options either did not possess a 5G library or were costly to use for this Praxis research. Therefore, the researcher considers CyberVAN limited in its cyber resilience testing capabilities. However, a simple method for simulating a denial-of-service (DoS) attack in CyberVAN exists.

A DoS attack in CyberVAN is simulated by running Python code on a network device. The code will inject a DoS attack to the subject element. The Linux code to perform the DoS injection is as follows:

```
van-dmz-tmc-1 ~]$ vi send_dos_attack.py
van-dmz-tmc-1 ~]$ python3 send_dos_attack.py 8 0
van-dmz-tmc-1 ~]$ python3 send_dos_attack.py 8 1
van-dmz-tmc-1 ~]$ python3 send_dos_attack.py 8 0
van-dmz-tmc-1 ~]$ python3 send_dos_attack.py 8 1
van-dmz-tmc-1 ~]$ python3 send_dos_attack.py 8 0
van-dmz-tmc-1 ~]$ python3 send_dos_attack.py 8 1
```

Figure 12. The Linux Commands to Inject the Denial-of-Service Attack in

CyberVAN.

To inject a DoS attack, the first step is to edit the "send_dos_attack.py" Python file. Injecting a DoS attack is contingent on two things: device ID and a zero value. The "8" in the figure above indicates the device ID that will experience the attack. The last value is binary. To inject the attack, the researcher entered "1", and "0" was entered to end the attack after the researcher assessed the attack's effect on the network. To discover the device

ID of the element, the author executed "ifconfig" in CyberVAN's command prompt. The device ID designations are shown in the figure below:

```
<!--AccessPoint-Backhaul has simulation id 0-->
<!--Enb-LocA has simulation id 1-->
<!--Enb-LocB has simulation id 2-->
<!--Gnb-LocC has simulation id 3-->
<!--Router-BackhaulA has simulation id 4-->
<!--Router-BackhaulB has simulation id 5-->
<!--Router-BackhaulC has simulation id 6-->
<!--Router-Core has simulation id 7-->
<!--Sgw-36 has simulation id 8-->
<!--Mme-37 has simulation id 9-->
<!--Pgw-38 has simulation id 10-->
<!--Switch-76 has simulation id 11-->
<!--Router-Backbone has simulation id 12-->
<!--remotehost has simulation id 13-->
```

Figure 13. The Device ID Designations after Executing the "ifconfig" Command.

In this case, "8" is identified as the SGW-36 network element of the LTE communication plane in the NSA Model that experienced the attack. To experiment, the author pinged the second Evolved UE device (eue2) from the first Evolved UE device (eue1). After the attack was injected into SGW-36, eue1 could not reach eue2 any further. The ping termination is illustrated below:

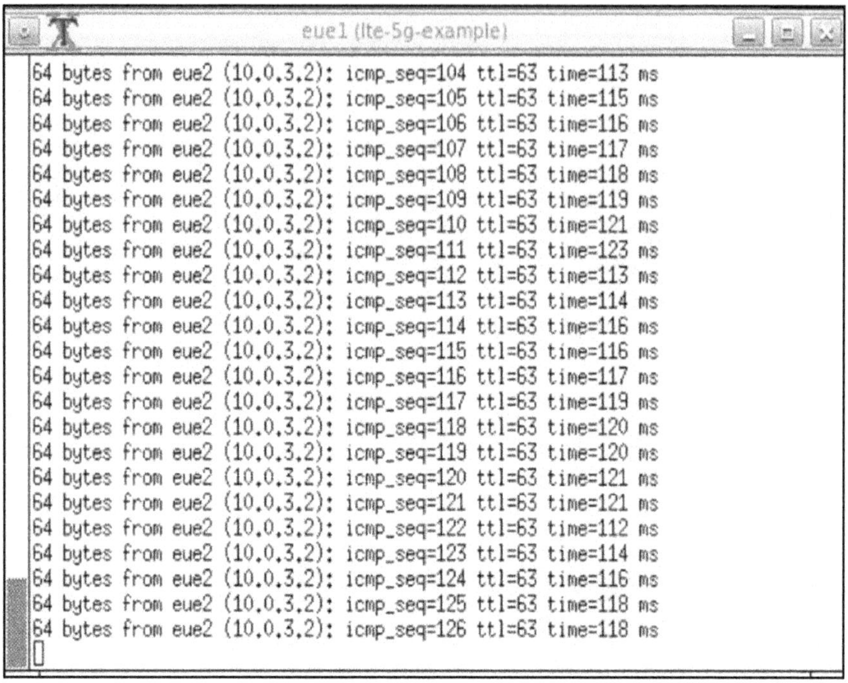

Figure 14. eue1-eue2 Ping Termination after Denial-of-Service Attack Injection. The communication link between eue1 and eue2 was broken because SGW manages the packet routing between the UE network, RAN, and CN. The DoS attack successfully compromised the SGW, which halted communication between the two user devices.

The author demonstrated the execution of a simple DoS attack in CyberVAN. However, the researcher could not test the cyber resilience of the architecture against the attack. Cyber resilience in CyberVAN is only possible when utilizing the Attack Sequence function, which is currently unavailable for use. Peraton Labs plans to make this function operational for a future software version of CyberVAN. Therefore, the researcher could not substantiate the notion that CyberVAN can conduct cyber resilience testing.

4.4 Hypothesis 3 Results

Hypothesis 3 (H3) reads as follows: "The Perimeter Security Model performs better in network latency." The researcher believes that this hypothesis will be substantiated because of the model's more straightforward design in comparison with the ZT Microsegmentation Model, which consists of a layered defense approach. The ping function in CyberVAN was used to assess the models' implications in network latency. The NSA architecture was utilized to facilitate substantiation of H1 and H2, and its network latency parameters will be documented in this section. The network latency results for the NSA Model will not influence the recommendations for the ideal architectural solution since it is a 5G topology and not a specified architecture model.

The ping function in CyberVAN was used to gauge the network latency. Below are CyberVAN ping results for the PS Model after using the Linux terminal of the first virtual machine (gue1) to ping the second virtual machine (gue2) and the Internet user (remotehost), respectively:

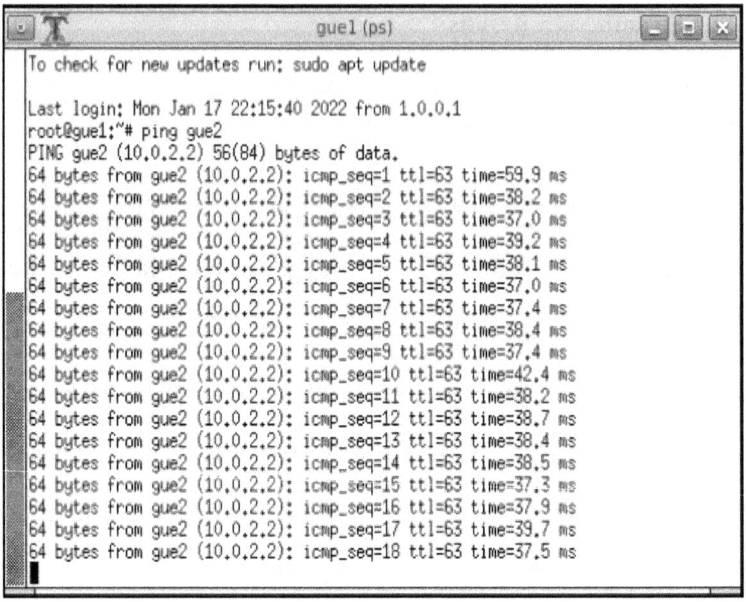

Figure 15. CyberVAN Perimeter Security Model Ping Results between gue1 and

gue2.

Figure 15 is the PS Model result of the researcher pinging gue2 from gue1. The author wanted to run a quick ping test with the other virtual machine before reaching the Internet user to ensure a connection with a nearby network device. No packet loss was reported, so 33 packets were transmitted and received. Below is the result of the author pinging

"remotehost" after the connection between both virtual machines was shown to be strong:

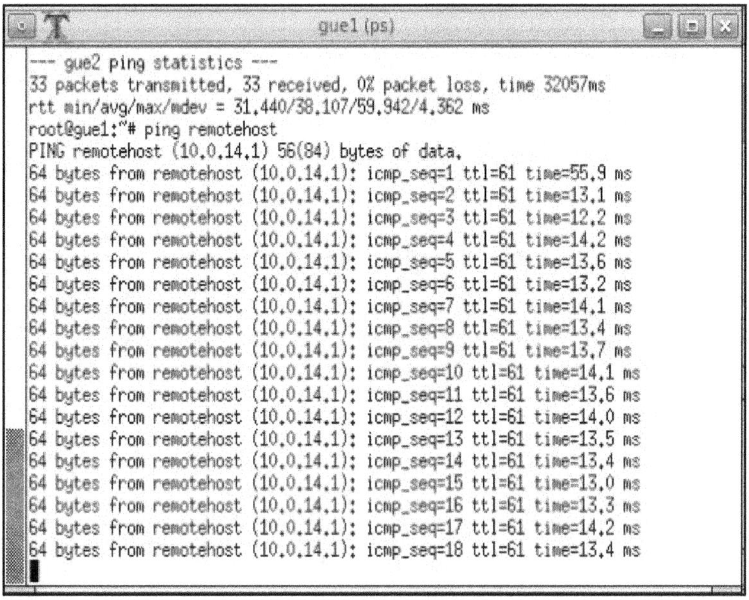

Figure 16. CyberVAN Perimeter Security Model Ping Results between gue1 and

remotehost.

Figure 16 is the PS Model result of the researcher pinging remotehost from gue1.

The ping range is from 12.2 to 14.2 milliseconds (ms) after the first delayed ping response, which are strong network performance results. Integrated Research (n.d.) states that the optimal ping range for a network is between 30 to 40 ms. The researcher concludes that the PS Model of this size produces optimal network performance results based on Integrated Research's recommended ping range. Below are CyberVAN ping results for the ZT Microsegmentation Model after using the Linux terminal of the first virtual machine (gue1) to ping the second virtual machine (gue2) and the Internet user (remotehost), respectively:

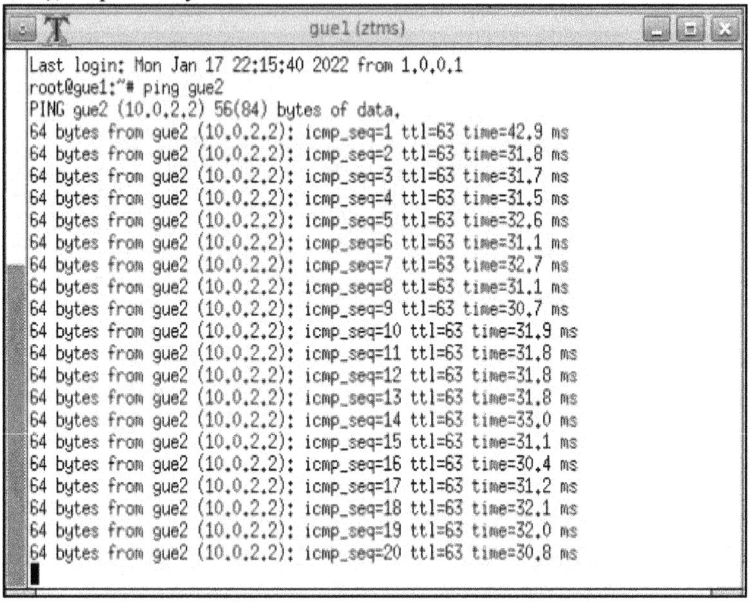

```
Last login: Mon Jan 17 22:15:40 2022 from 1.0.0.1
root@gue1:~# ping gue2
PING gue2 (10.0.2.2) 56(84) bytes of data.
64 bytes from gue2 (10.0.2.2): icmp_seq=1 ttl=63 time=42.9 ms
64 bytes from gue2 (10.0.2.2): icmp_seq=2 ttl=63 time=31.8 ms
64 bytes from gue2 (10.0.2.2): icmp_seq=3 ttl=63 time=31.7 ms
64 bytes from gue2 (10.0.2.2): icmp_seq=4 ttl=63 time=31.5 ms
64 bytes from gue2 (10.0.2.2): icmp_seq=5 ttl=63 time=32.6 ms
64 bytes from gue2 (10.0.2.2): icmp_seq=6 ttl=63 time=31.1 ms
64 bytes from gue2 (10.0.2.2): icmp_seq=7 ttl=63 time=32.7 ms
64 bytes from gue2 (10.0.2.2): icmp_seq=8 ttl=63 time=31.1 ms
64 bytes from gue2 (10.0.2.2): icmp_seq=9 ttl=63 time=30.7 ms
64 bytes from gue2 (10.0.2.2): icmp_seq=10 ttl=63 time=31.9 ms
64 bytes from gue2 (10.0.2.2): icmp_seq=11 ttl=63 time=31.8 ms
64 bytes from gue2 (10.0.2.2): icmp_seq=12 ttl=63 time=31.8 ms
64 bytes from gue2 (10.0.2.2): icmp_seq=13 ttl=63 time=31.8 ms
64 bytes from gue2 (10.0.2.2): icmp_seq=14 ttl=63 time=33.0 ms
64 bytes from gue2 (10.0.2.2): icmp_seq=15 ttl=63 time=31.1 ms
64 bytes from gue2 (10.0.2.2): icmp_seq=16 ttl=63 time=30.4 ms
64 bytes from gue2 (10.0.2.2): icmp_seq=17 ttl=63 time=31.2 ms
64 bytes from gue2 (10.0.2.2): icmp_seq=18 ttl=63 time=32.1 ms
64 bytes from gue2 (10.0.2.2): icmp_seq=19 ttl=63 time=32.0 ms
64 bytes from gue2 (10.0.2.2): icmp_seq=20 ttl=63 time=30.8 ms
```

Figure 17. CyberVAN Zero Trust Microsegmentation Model Ping Results between

gue1 and gue2.

Figure 17 is the ZT Microsegmentation Model result of the researcher pinging gue2 from gue1.

The researcher ran a quick ping test to the “gue2” virtual machine before reaching the Internet user to ensure a connection with a nearby network device. No packet loss was reported, so 28 packets were transmitted and received. Below is the result of the test pinging “remotehost”:

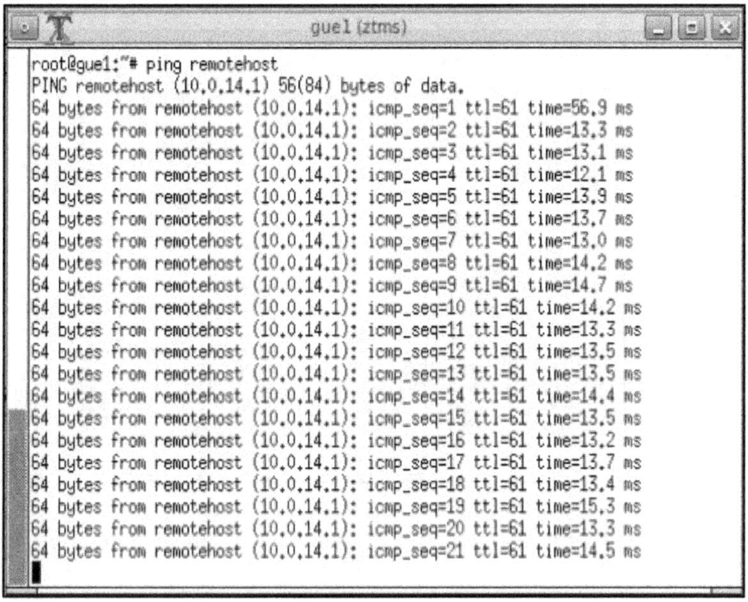

Figure 18. CyberVAN Zero Trust Microsegmentation Model Ping Results between

gue1 and remotehost.

Figure 18 is the ZT Microsegmentation Model result of the researcher pinging remotehost from gue1.

The researcher also simulated the alternate architecture showcased in Section 4.2.

The researcher was interested in comparing the results of this topology alongside the Perimeter Security and Zero Trust Microsegmentation Models because it incorporates an

LTE and NR profile. The ping results for this design are as follows:

```
64 bytes from remotehost (10.0.12.2): icmp_seq=12 ttl=62 time=31.7 ms
64 bytes from remotehost (10.0.12.2): icmp_seq=13 ttl=62 time=33.0 ms
64 bytes from remotehost (10.0.12.2): icmp_seq=14 ttl=62 time=23.7 ms
64 bytes from remotehost (10.0.12.2): icmp_seq=15 ttl=62 time=24.5 ms
64 bytes from remotehost (10.0.12.2): icmp_seq=16 ttl=62 time=25.6 ms
64 bytes from remotehost (10.0.12.2): icmp_seq=26 ttl=62 time=26.6 ms
64 bytes from remotehost (10.0.12.2): icmp_seq=27 ttl=62 time=27.8 ms
64 bytes from remotehost (10.0.12.2): icmp_seq=28 ttl=62 time=29.8 ms
64 bytes from remotehost (10.0.12.2): icmp_seq=29 ttl=62 time=31.2 ms
64 bytes from remotehost (10.0.12.2): icmp_seq=30 ttl=62 time=22.4 ms
64 bytes from remotehost (10.0.12.2): icmp_seq=31 ttl=62 time=24.7 ms
64 bytes from remotehost (10.0.12.2): icmp_seq=32 ttl=62 time=25.9 ms
64 bytes from remotehost (10.0.12.2): icmp_seq=33 ttl=62 time=26.9 ms
64 bytes from remotehost (10.0.12.2): icmp_seq=34 ttl=62 time=29.0 ms
64 bytes from remotehost (10.0.12.2): icmp_seq=35 ttl=62 time=30.8 ms
64 bytes from remotehost (10.0.12.2): icmp_seq=36 ttl=62 time=22.9 ms
64 bytes from remotehost (10.0.12.2): icmp_seq=37 ttl=62 time=23.2 ms
64 bytes from remotehost (10.0.12.2): icmp_seq=38 ttl=62 time=25.2 ms
64 bytes from remotehost (10.0.12.2): icmp_seq=39 ttl=62 time=26.7 ms
64 bytes from remotehost (10.0.12.2): icmp_seq=40 ttl=62 time=26.8 ms
64 bytes from remotehost (10.0.12.2): icmp_seq=41 ttl=62 time=29.1 ms
64 bytes from remotehost (10.0.12.2): icmp_seq=42 ttl=62 time=31.8 ms
64 bytes from remotehost (10.0.12.2): icmp_seq=43 ttl=62 time=25.0 ms
```

Figure 19: CyberVAN Non-Standalone Model Ping Results between eue1 and

the remotehost.

Latency is greater for this topology because the packets travel a greater distance and are transmitted wirelessly at nodes throughout the system. However, the results are still favorable according to Integrated Research (n.d.).

In comparing the network latency of the models, the author evaluated the ping results of each model between gue1 and remotehost. Furthermore, a statistical analysis was made after the author conducted the H3 latency tests. The Analysis of Variance

(ANOVA) calculations for all models are as follows:

PS	ZTMS	NSA	Anova: Single Factor						
13.1	13.3	31.7	Summary						
12.2	13.1	33	Groups	Count	Sum	Average	Variance		
14.2	12.1	23.7	PS	17	230	13.52941176	0.2659558824		
13.6	13.9	24.5	ZTMS	17	230.7	13.57058824	0.3709558824		
13.2	13.7	25.6	NSA	17	459.7	27.04117647	11.30007353		
14.1	13	26.6	Anova Test Results						
13.4	14.2	27.8	Source of Variation	SS	df	MS	F	P-value	F crit
13.7	14.7	29.8	Between Groups	2062.815294	2	1031.407647	259.2130982	0	3.190727336
14.1	14.2	31.2	Within Groups	190.9917647	48	3.978995098			
13.6	13.3	22.4	Total	2253.807059	50				
14	13.5	24.7	Tukey's Test						
13.5	13.5	25.9	Group Pairs	Absolute Difference	Standard Error	q_tukey			
13.4	14.4	26.9	PS vs. ZTMS	0.04117647059	0.4837959644	0.08511123204			
13	13.5	29	PS vs. NSA	13.51176471	0.4837959644	27.92864286			
13.3	13.2	30.8	ZTMS vs. NSA	13.47058824	0.4837959644	27.84353163			
14.2	13.7	22.9							
13.4	13.4	23.2							

Table 4. Tabulated Latency Results and Statistical Analysis of the Simulation

Models.

The latency results for each model are shown in Table 4 in the following order from left to right: PS Model (first column), ZT Microsegmentation Model (second column), and NSA Model (third column). Table 4 demonstrates that the PS Model edges the ZT Microsegmentation Model and produces more favorable results than the NSA Model in latency performance. Each model possesses a unique security profile; therefore, the Analysis of Variance (ANOVA) and Tukey tests are the analysis methods that will assess the statistical difference in network latency between each model. The researcher calculated the sums, means, variances, sum of squares (SS), degrees of freedom (DF), mean square (MS), F-statistic (F), probability value (p-value), critical F-value for the ANOVA test using Google Sheets mathematical algorithms. The sum of squares is calculated by adding the squared differences between each data point of the set and the dataset's mean. The degrees of freedom (df) represent the number of dataset values available to calculate a statistic. The df formula between groups is $k - 1$, where "k" is the number of groups or datasets. For within-groups, the formula is $N - k$, where “N” is the number of observations and “k” is still the number of groups. Lastly, the Tukey test was also conducted using Google Sheets to calculate the absolute difference, standard error, and the q-value. The mean square (MS) calculation is below: $MS = SS \div df$.

The F-statistic is commonly used in regression analysis and is a ratio of dataset variances.

The formula is as follows:

$F = (variation\ between\ group\ means) \div (variation\ within\ the\ groups)$. The

critical F value is a number of the F-statistic that establishes the threshold where the null hypothesis should be rejected. Lastly, the p-value is the chance of obtaining an F-statistic value greater than the computed one.

The ANOVA test was the statistical analysis selected by the researcher to determine if there is a significant difference between the PS, ZT Microsegmentation, and NSA Models. To conduct the test, the author must first set up the hypotheses. The null hypothesis (H0) indicates no significant difference between the metrics, and the alternative hypothesis (Ha) is the opposite of H0 where there is a significant difference between the metrics. The outcome of the ANOVA test is statistically significant if the calculated p-value is reported as less than the critical value (0.05), which means the null hypothesis should be rejected. However, the outcome is insignificant if the p-value is greater than the critical value, and the author should not reject the null hypothesis. The calculated p-value shown in Table 4 is zero, which indicates that the data matches the null hypothesis. Therefore, the difference in network latency between the three architecture models is statistically significant.

Tukey's test must be conducted to identify where a significant difference exists between the data groups. The mathematical algorithms of Google Sheets were used to calculate the absolute difference, standard error, and q values. The absolute difference is the absolute value of mean differences between groups. In turn, the outcome is compared to the critical value, also known as the Honestly Significant Difference (HSD). This metric is essential because it helps determine whether the difference between datasets is statistically significant. There were three group pairs established to calculate the absolute difference values. The group pairs are as follows: PS vs. ZTMS, PS vs. NSA, and ZTMS vs. NSA. The absolute difference formulas for each group pair are shown below: $|\underline{PS} - \underline{ZTMS}|$, $|\underline{PS} - \underline{NSA}|$, and $|\underline{ZTMS} - NSA|$. As a result, the absolute difference between the PS and Zero Trust Microsegmentation (ZTMS) Models is small at 0.04; however, it is comparable when assessing the PS vs. NSA (13.51) and ZTMS vs. NSA (13.47) group pairs. The standard error will be equivalent for the three group pairs, and its formula is as follows: $Standard\ Error = \sqrt{MSE \div Count}$, where Mean Square Error (MSE) is the MS within groups value, and Count is the number of data points for each set, which is 17. The outcome is 0.48 for all group pairs. Lastly, the q-value formula

is the following: $Absolute\ Difference \div Standard\ Error$. The q-values for the PS vs.

ZTMS, PS vs. NSA, and ZTMS vs. NSA pairs are 0.09, 27.93, and 27.84, respectively.

Purdue University (n.d.) published the "Critical Values of Studentized Range Distribution" document that includes the critical q-values depending on the corresponding df value and number of groups, which is three. To identify the critical qvalue for this use case, the researcher must use the df within groups value of 48 to locate the critical q-value. After reviewing the source, the author determined that the critical qvalue is 3.42. The calculated q-values for the PS vs. NSA and ZTMS vs. NSA pairs are much larger than 3.42, which denotes that the difference in means is statistically significant. However, the PS vs. ZTMS group pair is lower than the critical value, indicating that the difference in means between the datasets is not statistically significant, and there is enough evidence to reject the null hypothesis. The null hypothesis is accepted after assessing the other two group pairs.

4.5 Conclusion

In conclusion, the architecture models were successfully designed and meet the objectives and requirements mentioned in Section 3.2. The limitation was that CyberVAN's Attack Sequence function was not operational, so the researcher could not analyze the architectures' cyber resilience against the DoS attack. Furthermore, the substantiation of the hypotheses declared in Chapter 1 and Section 3.1 was still successful despite the limitation that influenced different strategies in answering Hypothesis 2 (H2) and Hypothesis 3 (H3). For Hypothesis 1 (H1), the various simulation models were designed to substantiate that the UE-NR system was the most effective topology for completing the scope of work. However, CyberVAN could not enhance the security resilience of the 5G network (H2). For Hypothesis 2 (H2) and Hypothesis 3 (H3), the researcher performed quantitative and statistical assessments to substantiate them. The Perimeter Security and Zero Trust Microsegmentation Models were compared, and based on the assessments, both models performed similarly during the network latency test. After extensive research, it was surprising that the ZT Microsegmentation Model was similar in network latency performance due to the model's increased complexity. The author also performed a statistical analysis of the resulting data for H3 by conducting an ANOVA test. After designing various architecture models, the ANOVA test results substantiated that statistically significant data existed for two network latency datasets out of three. The PS vs. ZTMS latency dataset was the only one deemed not statistically significant. The researcher does acknowledge that the ZT Microsegmentation Model is not a realistic solution today since HHS must call for ZT to be implemented, similar to what the DoD CIO did in 2022. More on these findings in Chapter 5. Therefore, the healthcare industry must implement the PS Model with a Defense-in-Depth (DiD) approach until the ZT policy is officially released by HHS. The NSA Model in Section 4.2 demonstrates DiD because it includes next-generation routers with firewall functionality. This capability was encompassed in the simulation code for the NSA Model. According to Fortinet (2024), DiD is "Defense-in-depth is a strategy that leverages multiple security measures to protect an organization's assets. The thinking is that if one line of defense is compromised, additional layers exist as a backup to ensure that threats are stopped along the way." Some additional measures that should be performed to enhance security include strong passwords, antivirus software, patch management, multi-factor authentication (MFA), etc. The benefit of ZT that DiD does not possess is the elimination of implicit trust. The author encourages a DiD approach for today's healthcare industry but ZT for the future.

Chapter 5—Discussion and Conclusions

5.1 Discussion

After recording the test results of each hypothesis in Chapter 4, the researcher found the research to be successful and productive. Before deciding on the ideal security architecture between the PS and ZT Microsegmentation Models, the author had to evaluate the unique 5G topology model. The researcher determined that the current UENR and NSA topologies were optimal in producing simulation results for this Praxis. The restatement of the research questions and hypotheses is mentioned in the next section, in addition to the summary of major findings for each hypothesis. Lastly, cybersecurity architecture policy recommendations for the healthcare sector will be explained later in this chapter.

5.2 Conclusions

In this section, the researcher will revisit the research questions and hypotheses that were tested and designate the major findings and key takeaways from the research conducted to substantiate them. The research questions (RQs) and hypotheses (Hs) are as follows:

RQ1: Which network topology (User Equipment-Radio Network Access, User

Equipment-New Radio) in CyberVAN is most effective in completing the scope of work?

RQ2: Can CyberVAN enhance the security resilience of the 5G architecture?

RQ3: Does the Perimeter Security, Zero Trust Microsegmentation, or Non-

Standalone Model perform better in network latency?

H1: The User Equipment-New Radio topology in CyberVAN is most effective in completing the scope of work.

H2: CyberVAN will enhance the security resilience of the 5G architecture.

H3: The Perimeter Security Model performs better in network latency.

For H1, the author in Chapter 4 elaborated on why the UE-NR topology was deemed to be the optimal system to complete the scope of work. The UE-RAN topology was one of the 5G models available for design in CyberVAN but caused trouble in simulating the architecture. At the same time, the UE-NR system was able to simulate due to additional 5G properties included in the NR channel that was not in the UE-RAN design. The other critical factor is CyberVAN, based on network type consideration, learning curve, scalability, and license cost, which was selected as the ideal network simulator for this Praxis but did not possess much cyber resiliency testing capability. For H2, CyberVAN could not substantiate that it can improve security resilience for the healthcare use case. CyberVAN can simulate an attack such as DoS but is not currently able to test cyber resilience. The author recommends that another researcher utilize a more capable network simulator for testing a system's cyber resilience. For H3, the researcher conducted an ANOVA test comparing the network latency metrics for the PS, ZT Microsegmentation, and NSA Models. As a result, the PS vs. ZTMS metrics were deemed not statistically significant, but the PS vs. NSA and ZTMS vs. NSA comparisons were found statistically significant.

Another conclusion that was made after the researcher completed the methodology was that NIST's Cybersecurity Framework (CSF) 2.0 is the best risk management cycle for the healthcare sector to leverage due to the Organizational Profile and Community Profile. These profiles contain a wide range of sensitive information, including PCI, PHI, and PII. Healthcare is one of the few industries that have an Organizational Profile and Community Profile of at least three critical data types, which makes the industry an attractive target to cyber attackers. The author detailed how a healthcare corporation would build the CSF 2.0 Organization Profile. The Community Profile is a collection of Organizational Profiles reflecting a healthcare network of several hospitals and clinics.

The last conclusions that the researcher made were security architecture policy recommendations for the use case. The author is calling for the federal authorizing body of the healthcare sector, i.e., HHS, to collaborate with CISA to develop the strategy for 5G use. HHS, with the help of CISA, should section the strategy as follows: Executive Summary, Introduction, Strategic Goals & Objectives, HHS Zero Trust Approach, and Conclusion (DoD CIO, 2022, p. 6). Section 3.8 recommends content that should be included under the Introduction section; however, the researcher will suggest content for the other sections of the strategy.

For Strategic Goals & Objectives, there should be four goals: Zero Trust Mindset Adoption, Cyber-Resilient Information Systems, Accelerated Technology Deployment, and Zero Trust Realization. Goal #1, Zero Trust Mindset Adoption, promotes a way of thinking that directs the architecture's development and implementation (DoD CIO, 2022, p. 12). The entire healthcare sector is trained and educated on every individual's responsibility in protecting critical assets. Objective initiatives for this goal include training, outreach, commitment, etc. Goal #2, Cyber-Resilient Information Systems, ensures that system components apply to the ZT framework to all legacy and new healthcare information systems to operationalize ZT to achieve enterprise resilience. Objective initiatives for this goal include user, device, applications and workloads, network and environment, etc. (DoD CIO, 2022, p. 12). Goal #3, Accelerated Technology Deployment, launches ZT-based systems at a pace equal to industry advancements at a minimum by leveraging cutting-edge technologies that fail and enhance quickly for innovation. Objective initiatives for this goal include capabilities, interoperability, innovation, etc. (DoD CIO, 2022, p. 12). Goal #4, Zero Trust Realization, guarantees that procedures, guidelines, and resources are incorporated into the ZT execution, producing a coordinated ZT architectural framework. Objective initiatives for this goal include planning, funding, performance, policy, etc. (DoD CIO, 2022, p. 13).

The HHS Zero Trust Approach section details the assumptions and principles that are established in realizing the strategy's vision. Several assumptions will be established; however, there are two that must be added to the list. The first assumption pertaining to

ZT implementation is that it is about culture and not just technology (DoD CIO, 2022, p.

7). This is important to understand because technology is thought to uphold cybersecurity. The general public, including cyber experts, tends to forget that the weakest link in cybersecurity is the human factor. This is where encouraging a culture of thorough security training, education, policy, and other imperative security controls is important for an industry like healthcare that handles sensitive data. The second assumption is leadership and healthcare worker buy-in is mandatory (DoD CIO, 2022, p. 8). ZT does not solely fall under the accountability of the Information Technology (IT) team. The architecture can only be successfully maintained if buy-in from all components and departments of corporations is established. Every component and department must also understand its role in sustaining a successful ZT environment. There are different categories of principles, such as technical and governance. A technical principle would include least privilege where an entity is only allowed a privilege needed for it to complete tasks. However, a governance principle includes a "never trust, always verify" mentality for every user and device. Implicit trust that exists in a traditional cybersecurity model does not exist in ZTA. Lastly, the Conclusion summarizes the subjects discussed in the strategy and how effective it will be for the healthcare industry if buy-in from leadership and healthcare workers is established.

After the HHS and CISA collaboration is complete, there should be a finished publication elaborating on the future approach for the author's recommended cybersecurity architectural solution titled "Healthcare Zero Trust Strategy." The DoD CIO ZT Strategy that was released in November

2022 and yielded from the 2022 National Defense Strategy is a template for the HHS and CISA to compose a similar strategy for the healthcare sector. HHS should also collaborate with the DoD CIO since the office has already enforced a timeline for the ZT architecture to be deployed in the defense industry. The DoD gave a five-year period for the industry to plan and implement the strategy before it was fully operational. For the healthcare sector, the researcher finds it reasonable to grant a five-year transitional period similar to what the DoD CIO ZT Strategy expected for the Defense Industry. However, this will go into effect after the HHS memorandum is released to inform the public about the upcoming strategy release. Therefore, the Healthcare ZT Strategy should be deployed by the beginning of FY2030 or October 1, 2029.

5.3 Contributions to Body of Knowledge

After Praxis completion, the researcher provided the following contributions to the specified research area:

1. Compared different 5G architectures modeled in CyberVAN and evaluated the security profile and network latency implications of each model.
2. Composed guidance on how to apply NIST Cybersecurity Framework (CSF) 2.0 as the risk management and continuous improvement cycle for a healthcare corporation to enable the implementation of dynamic security measures

3. Introduce 5G cybersecurity architecture policy recommendations for the healthcare sector so that an architectural vision is established based on the researcher's key findings

One of the research objectives mentioned in Chapter 1 was to encourage Industry to conduct extensive architectural research in order to enhance the mobile network's resilience in preparation for both 5G SA and 6G deployment. Based on the author's findings, the reader should now be clear on why 5G architectural research is essential in solutioning the growing number of vulnerabilities as the mobile network continues to expand in capacity and capability.

5.4 Recommendations for Future Research

After completion of this Praxis, the researcher documented some future work recommendations to satisfy the dire need of a cyber-resilient security architecture for the 5G mobile network detailed in Chapter 1. The future research recommendations are as follows:

- Utilize a more capable network simulator to facilitate cyber resilience testing of cybersecurity architectures
- Conduct research on efficient ways of how to secure 5G networks with the cloudbased core network, the 5G Standalone topology
- Apply different business use cases and simulate their corresponding architecture scenarios to resolve unique cybersecurity challenges for each use case

www.ingramcontent.com/pod-product-compliance
Lightning Source LLC
Chambersburg PA
CBHW071355230926
51846CB00002B/567
* 9 7 8 3 8 5 2 2 3 9 3 3 0 *